WELCOME TO WITNESS

Becoming an evangelising parish

Paul Cannon & Sharon Beech

CONTENTS

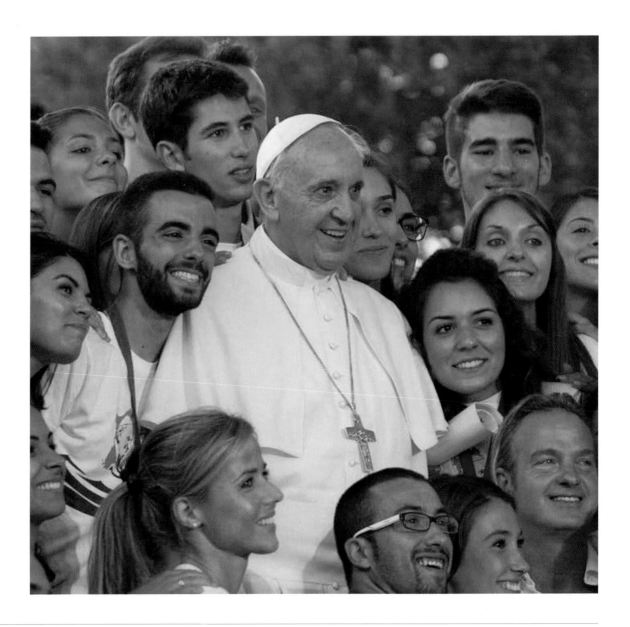

BIOGRAPHIES

Paul Cannon was ordained priest for the Diocese of Salford in 1982. In 1987 he was appointed a team member of the Catholic Missionary Society based in London, and from 1991-1994 he served as its director. On completion of his term of office at CMS he studied for his master's degree in adult religious education at Loyola University, Chicago. He is currently the parish priest of Our Lady of Good Counsel and Guardian Angels in Bury, Lancashire, and Episcopal Vicar for Evangelisation for Salford Diocese. Over the past few years he has been a regular contributor to Redemptorist Publications.

Sharon Beech is Project Development Co-ordinator for the Department for Evangelisation for Salford Diocese. A mother of three and grandmother to five, Sharon has worked for Salford Diocese for eighteen years, firstly as a parish office administrator and in recent years for the Department for Evangelisation. She has a bachelor's and master's degree in theology and religious studies and has written on the impact of Christianity on the Inuit and the anthropology of ritual in a secular society. She has also written articles for Paulist evangelisation ministries in Washington DC.

FOREWORDS

Archbishop Bernard Longley

*I*n October 2012, I was privileged to be part of the Synod on the New Evangelisation which was called by Pope Benedict XVI and coincided with the Year of Faith. The Synod took place 7-28 October and the Year of Faith began on the 11 October. We all arrived at the Synod with great enthusiasm. As we, the bishops, started our deliberations, we knew that we carried with us the enthusiasm of the people, not only in my own Archdiocese of Birmingham, but also from all the dioceses throughout England and Wales. We were aware of being united with the Holy Father and the other bishops of the Church who had gathered for this Synod.

Evangelisation is the central mission of the Church and successive popes have made this the core of their apostolate.

St John XXIII instigated the Second Vatican Council and called for the windows of the Church to be opened.

Blesssed Pope Paul VI, after the Synod on Evangelisation in 1974, produced the definitive Exhortation on Evangelisation, *Evangelii Nuntiandi*. This document was to breathe new life into the work of evangelisation. It opened up the Church to a new way of thinking about how, when and to whom we are to bring the Good News of Jesus Christ.

Next, St John Paul II was to bring a new hope to the Church. He encouraged us to look closely at a "New Evangelisation", reaching out to our neighbours and recognizing in them a brotherhood and sisterhood in Christ.

More recently Pope Benedict set up the Pontifical Council for the New Evangelisation and moved its work forward by calling for a Synod on the New Evangelisation in 2012.

With the resignation of Pope Benedict, Pope Francis has moved us into an even greater era for evangelisation with his exhortation, *Evangelii Gaudium*. This document is a blueprint for the future. In so many ways, it has inspired us to work towards a greater understanding of each other and of our uniqueness in the world.

Pope Francis has thrown down a gauntlet to the whole Church. There is a new enthusiasm among the people to be new evangelisers. This can only be the work of the Holy Spirit, the same Spirit who guided the Synod of Bishops with the Holy Father; the same Spirit who is drawing these good things from the people within our parishes.

Bishop Terence Brain

Fr Paul Cannon and Mrs Sharon Beech, from the Department for Evangelisation in Salford Diocese, have picked up that gauntlet. They have worked for several years to encourage and support those who want to advance the work of evangelisation within their own parishes. This book will enable many people, both clergy and lay, to devise new and imaginative ways of spreading the Good News of Jesus Christ. As evangelisers we must not be afraid to reach out to the world. We must welcome the enriching presence of others into the life of the Church, accepting and delighting in them as we confidently sow the seeds of growth.

Scripture gives us many examples of the way in which Jesus welcomes the outsider, making disciples of the marginalised and healing the wounded. In our mission we should be the healers, bringing new life and hope to those who need it; bringing the message of God's personal love wherever it is needed. What was it that moved God to send his only Son to die for us, so that we could live again?

I hope that this book can be a productive resource for all who want to reach out with that same healing love. May it help to bring the Gospel message afresh to those inside our Church and beyond our parish communities, to all those who seek the presence of the Lord in their lives.

+Bernard Longley
Archbishop of Birmingham
Member of the Pontifical Council
for Promoting the New Evangelisation

*H*aving knowledge and being able to impart it to others do not always go together. Good teachers have this skill, but not all teachers have it: there is an art in communicating knowledge and inspiring others to receive and develop it.

What I like about this book is its simplicity and clarity: it teaches practical ways to "put out into the deep and to let down the net" as St John Paul II invited us to do in his encyclical for the new millennium, *Novo Millennio Ineunte*. This call to go out and proclaim the Gospel was underlined in the teaching of Pope Benedict XVI, who spoke of those "without hope" because they do not know Christ. We put out into the deep to bring Christ's redemptive love (*Spe Salvi*, 2007).

And now Pope Francis has called on all of us to reach out with the joy of the Gospel to all men and women so that they might live in hope (*Evangelii Gaudium, 2013*).

The teaching of our recent popes is to be found throughout this book. It is a fine pastoral resource, enabling individuals and communities and parishes to decide how and where to "let down the net" that Christ has entrusted to them. Enjoy the adventure.

+Terence J. Brain
Bishop Emeritus of Salford

INTRODUCTION

What is evangelisation?

Someone who is thinking of becoming a Catholic in our parish recently asked us, "What is evangelisation?" We gave what we thought was a succinct answer: "Proclaiming the Gospel message to other people through word and action." The response, however, came as a complete surprise: "Really? Do you mean Catholics do that?"

We certainly do! In fact this is central to our identity and mission as the Church. Without sharing the Gospel message, the Church will die. The word "evangelisation" has often been regarded as a technical term and we have shied away from using it. But things are changing. The Year of Faith, which ended in 2013, began with the 2012 Synod of Bishops on the New Evangelisation (and they did not try to use another word!).

St John Paul II, Pope Benedict XVI and Pope Francis have all spoken about the urgency of re-discovering and celebrating our faith. We must, then, reach out to people who are or were part of the Church and need help to reawaken their faith. We must also turn to those searching for new meaning in their lives. St John Paul II first coined the phrase "the new evangelisation"; Pope Benedict called a Synod on that same theme; Pope Francis is encouraging all of us to "go out and do it"!

But how do we do "it"?
By becoming an evangelising parish!
This book, *Welcome to Witness: Becoming an evangelising parish,* is for everyone in the parish. Our parishes must be places where the sharing of the Gospel message is our main priority. This should be automatic! We must have open, family-friendly and welcoming parishes. We cannot hold the attitude that "they know where we are if they ever need us". Those who have fallen away from the regular practice of their faith, or those who are not yet members of the Church, are the very people we are meant to reach out to. Where they are, we must be also – be it in our work places, in our schools, in sports clubs, wherever. Wherever people gather, "they" are there. When the opportunities arise, and they surely will, we must not be afraid to let them know that we are members of the Church, and that the Church and our parish church is for them.

In our parishes do we openly encourage our fellow parishioners to be involved in sharing their faith with others and reaching out to them? In our parish at the beginning of Advent and Lent we launch a prayer and action campaign. We invite people to begin the season by lighting a candle in church for someone they would either like to see return to the Church or come for the first time. Having lit a candle for them, we then invite our parishioners to pray daily during the season for that person, and then, as either Christmas or Easter approaches, to invite the person they have been praying for to come to church with them. People find it so much easier to come into a strange place when there is someone there to guide them. This is a simple example of enabling people in the pews to reach out.

We also try to give people in the pews a voice, or at least a small column in the weekly newsletter. We ask for volunteers to write a small piece for each week's newsletter, entitled 'A view from the pew'. We don't expect (or want) a theological treatise, just a simple reflection on the Sunday Gospel or a specific feast, from the perspective of an ordinary parishioner who is trying to understand what the Gospel message is saying to them. We keep the "view from the pew" anonymous, and over the many years that we have been doing this, we haven't uncovered any heresies!

In parish life (and this is where most people find an expression of what it means to be a Catholic), we have key moments when there are people present who could be the returning Catholics of the future or new members of the Church. But a lot depends on us and our attitude. Key moments in people's lives which still bring them into contact with us in church are births (baptisms), marriages and deaths. The liturgies that we celebrate with people at these times will either attract them or distance them from us. The follow-up we provide, the words we speak, our very presence at these key moments, could radically change their view of the Church. Our actions can help people to see that we are enacting the command of Jesus to love one another.

In the following chapters we will be exploring how we can take steps to awaken in our parish communities – and in the lives of individuals – the call to evangelise. We must be looking for all possible opportunities to share our faith and pass on the Gospel message. It starts with parents, but doesn't stop there. The responsibility of the whole Church is to be there to support and guide parents in this work, through our parishes and through our schools.

We must open our church doors, invite and welcome people, and share our faith with them. If they see a joyful expression on our faces, they might want to join us. If they are ignored or find a church that is exactly the same as the one they left, they will remain outside. As Pope Francis said in his homily on 24 July 2013 at the Basilica of the Shrine of Our Lady of Aparecida in Brazil: "Christians are joyful; they are never gloomy... Christians cannot be pessimists! They do not look like someone in constant mourning."

As Catholics we are called to engage with the culture around us, share our ideals and values: people will notice that we are identifiable by the love we share with anyone open to receiving it.

We are constantly told that our country is "post-Christian"; yet not all of our churches are empty and people do turn to them at key moments in their lives. We have to have the desire to share the Good News, to tell the story of Jesus whenever the opportunity arises, and always be welcoming and inviting.

Many recent Church documents make it clear that lay people have a unique and irreplaceable presence in the secular world. The witness of a Christian life, acts of charity and working for justice are as vital and urgent today as at any time in history.

As the Church, and as the local Church in our diocese and parish, we must be enabling and encouraging people to do these things.

We hope that, through the chapters of this book, you will find inspiration and ideas as individuals and as parish communities, so that our parishes may truly become places of welcome and witness.

CHAPTER ONE

Where we were:

from the 1974 Synod on Evangelisation to Evangelii Nuntiandi

Have you ever tried to trace your family history? You probably know when and where you were born, but what about your parents, grandparents and great-grandparents? What is their story? How did your ancestors live and what were their hopes and dreams? How did previous generations help to make you who you are today? A family tree helps us to discover our identity and where we have come from: it helps us to tell our story.

Just as important moments moulded our human family, so also with the spiritual family of the Church. From time to time, a flash of inspiration led the Church in a new direction and generated fresh insight and energy. Such experiences translated the Gospel message for different ages, cultures and societies. In this way, when people declare, "We want to see Jesus," the Church can reply, in countless languages, "This is Jesus."

Evangelisation is nothing more and nothing less than pointing to the presence of Jesus in the reality of people's lives through their own language, culture, traditions and experiences.

Key moments

In terms of evangelisation, what might be the key moments in the story of the Church?

Obviously, we must start with Jesus. Before his return to the Father, he gave his disciples and, therefore, the Church,

his final missionary command: "Make disciples of all the nations; baptise them in the name of the Father and of the Son and of the Holy Spirit, and teach them to observe all the commands I gave you." (Matthew 28:19)

We are a missionary Church because it is rooted in the final command of Jesus our Lord. Jesus did not stay inside the confines of sacred space; he went out to meet people, teaching them by the seashore, on hilltops, in the market-places, in their houses. Jesus used every opportunity available to him, even when he was dying on the cross, to proclaim his liberating Gospel message. This energetic people-loving Jesus is our model for evangelisation.

Across the centuries Church councils and local synods provided many other important milestones.

Some important modern initiatives for evangelisation

- **The Second Vatican Council:** This took place from 1962 until 1965 and changed the face of the Church, refocusing our vision on its mission.
- **The Synod of Bishops:** As one of its outcomes, the Second Vatican Council introduced the Synod of Bishops, an advisory body for the pope composed of bishops from across the world. They meet regularly to consider important questions about the activity and future direction of the Church.

- **The Synod on Evangelisation in the Modern World:** In 1974, the Third Ordinary Synod of Bishops focused on "evangelisation" and made it an urgent priority for the Church throughout the world. Suddenly, a word scarcely used in the documents of Vatican II became the focus for this international gathering of bishops.

- ***Evangelii Nuntiandi:*** Following Vatican II and the Synod on Evangelisation, Blessed Pope Paul VI produced this ground-breaking encyclical in 1975. Theologians and missionaries regard this encyclical as one of the great works to influence and challenge the Church. It has since shaped and inspired the entire evangelising activity of the Church, including Pope Francis' Apostolic Exhortation of 2013, *Evangelii Gaudium.*

Theory into practice

It is all very well to say that the Church needs to "get out there and do it", but there can be a big gap between theory and practice. The Gospel message must be translated into many languages; it must be planted and rooted in different societies and cultures if it is to be a source of life for everyone.

After Vatican II, bishops from across the world needed to come together to consider what it meant, within their own context, to "make disciples of all the nations". The 1974 Synod on Evangelisation was the first such assembly in modern times. *Evangelii Nuntiandi* was the response to their deliberations.

The Church's mission is a two-way process of sending and receiving. At the beginning of the Synod in 1974 Blessed Pope Paul VI placed the entire work of the Synod under the direction of the Holy Spirit as a sign of unity; all the members sought to be worthy to communicate God's peace and salvation to the world. He challenged the bishops at the Synod on Evangelisation to reflect both on their sending and the receivers of the message. Almost forty years later, this remains vital for any parish seeking to be transformed and become truly missionary.

Today the Church is even more aware that evangelisation must consider and reflect the cultural and social context in which people live, work and act today.

Blessed Pope Paul VI did not consider evangelisation to be an optional invitation for the Church. Without exception, all people, races and civilisations need to hear the Gospel message. Evangelisation and human progress complement each other and serve the same end: the salvation of humanity.

Pope Francis expresses similar thoughts throughout *Evangelii Gaudium*.

Interpreting the message

The 1974 Synod provided an occasion for reflection and writing on evangelisation in the modern world. If the Church is essentially missionary, every Christian has a duty to bear witness to Christ. But what does this mean in widely differing cultural and social contexts?

> *"Every Christian has a duty to bear witness to Christ."*

The Asian bishops, constantly encountering non-Christian religions, stressed the need for a new method and form of evangelisation: a dialogue through culture. Yet their situation differed from that in many Western countries, where Christianity had once flourished but where Christians are now in the minority.

There are, therefore, two important thrusts to evangelisation today. They both need a special and tailored approach:

- Taking the Gospel to places where it has never been heard (*primary evangelisation*).
- Taking the Gospel to places where it was once strong but has now been obscured or has disappeared altogether (*secondary evangelisation* or *re-evangelisation*).

At the same time, the Church cannot afford to neglect the needs of practising believers: they also need support and love if their faith is to flourish.

Changing times and changing needs

Evangelisation happens because the word is proclaimed – but who are the messengers of the Gospel in today's world?

In the early 1970s, the religious world was a very different place: there were many more priests; seminaries and religious houses were full, sometimes to bursting. Yet changes were already happening. It was vital to look towards the future. In reading the signs of the times in *Evangelii Nuntiandi*, Blessed Pope Paul VI addressed the question of the roles and responsibilities of clergy (paragraph 68). If evangelisation happens because the word is proclaimed, Blessed Pope Paul VI called on lay people, situated in the midst of the world, to grasp their special responsibilities with eagerness and faith.

Why and why not?

Why do people not practise their faith? What prevents them engaging with the local church community? The 1974 Synod discussed "non-practising Catholics" and "evangelisation in reference to ecumenism". Today there are still pressures on people, but perhaps the pressures are slightly different. Perhaps, compared to the 1970s, the rise in secularisation plays a larger part in the decline of church-going Catholics.

Dialogue

Through the influence of Vatican II, the Church has made significant progress in its dialogue with non-Christian religions and atheistic ideologies, becoming more open and understanding. St John Paul II's invitation, in 1986, to the leaders of the world faiths to join him in Assisi in order to pray for world peace exemplified the changing climate. He said:

I see this gathering today as a very significant sign of the commitment of all of you to the cause of peace. It is this commitment that has brought us to Assisi. The fact that we profess different creeds does not detract from the significance of this day. On the contrary, the Churches, Ecclesial Communities and World Religions are showing that they are eager for the good of humanity... Religions are many and varied, and they reflect the desire of men and women through the ages to enter into a relationship with the Absolute Being.

"Outreach is central to the vocation of all the baptised."

Mass media

Importantly for the Church, mass media, and personal and social communications have changed almost beyond recognition since the 1970s, opening up new opportunities for evangelisation in today's world.

What has been done? What remains to be done?

The Synod enabled bishops to share their experience of evangelisation and its effectiveness in their own countries. They asked what had been done and what could be done in the future.

The Synod and the subsequent document, *Evangelii Nuntiandi*, started a new movement in the Church. It placed evangelisation under the spotlight, highlighting this outreach as central to the vocation of all the baptised.

In the following chapters we will see how many of the topics discussed at the 1974 Synod are still on the agenda today for any parish (and individual) interested in evangelisation and mission.

CHAPTER TWO

Where we are now:

from Evangelii Nuntiandi to the present day

(St John Paul II, Pope Benedict XVI and the 2012 Synod of Bishops)

*F*rom the time of the 1974 Synod of Bishops on Evangelisation and Pope Paul VI's encyclical in 1975, *Evangelii Nuntiandi*, the word "evangelisation" and the phrase "the new evangelisation" have certainly entered into the Catholic vocabulary.

The 1974 Synod posed three questions for the Church:

- In our day, what has happened to that hidden energy of the Good News which is able to have a powerful effect on a person's conscience?
- To what extent and in what way can that evangelical force transform the people of this century?
- What methods should be followed in order that the power of the Gospel may have its effect?

These three questions are still valid many years later. However, just as the Church is constantly changing, so too, the world in which the Church lives and witnesses is continually altering, relentlessly creating new questions and challenges. The Church still needs to provide the answers. The Good News is still a hidden and transformative energy in people's lives that has not been fully exploited.

The new evangelisation

In the years since the 1974 Synod and *Evangelii Nuntiandi* there has been a reawakening in the Church of the urgency and importance of evangelisation.

Making it a focus of his pontificate, St John Paul II encouraged Catholics to evangelise in the spirit of the Second Vatican Council and Pope Paul VI. He was acutely aware of the fact that evangelisation occurs most effectively when the Church engages with the culture of those to whom she carries the Gospel message.

In June 1979, in his first visit as pope to his homeland, St John Paul ll was speaking in Nowa Hutta – a new town for workers constructed by the communist authorities – when he called for a new evangelisation, although he offered no details of his proposal. On 9 March 1983, while addressing the Catholic Bishops of Latin America at their General Assembly in Port-au-Prince, Haiti, St John Paul II called again for a "new evangelisation". This time he invited the Church to a new and "renewed" proclamation of the Gospel message. He called for new "ardour, methods and expressions" of evangelisation, ones that engage the society, culture and people of today. This time, people took notice of his invitation.

Evangelisation in action
Redemptoris Missio, the 1990 Encyclical of St John Paul II, marked the twenty-fifth anniversary of the Vatican II decree, *Ad Gentes*. It further developed the Church's spirituality and practice of evangelisation.

In his encyclical, the Pope focused on three specific circumstances in evangelisation:

• Preaching to those who have never heard the Gospel
• Preaching to those Christian communities where the Church is present, alive and active
• Preaching to those ancient, long-established Christian communities who "have lost a living sense of the faith, or even no longer consider themselves members of the Church, and live a life far removed from Christ and his Gospel"

During his pontificate, St John Paul II continued to refer to 'the new evangelisation' in his addresses and in his writings. His writings especially reveal certain central themes of his understanding of the new evangelisation including the implementation of the call

"The Gospel and the Church must confront the cultural crisis brought on by the world's increasing secularisation."

of the Second Vatican Council to proclaim the Good News of Jesus Christ by engagement with the present culture and to accompany individuals on their journey from this life to eternal life. St John Paul II stressed that the proclamation of the Gospel has first to be heard, secondly applied to one's own life, and that this will then result in conversion:

The proclamation of the Word of God has Christian conversion as its aim… conversion means accepting, by a personal decision, the saving sovereignty of Christ and becoming his disciple. (Redemptoris Missio, 46)

In his document *Christifideles Laici* (1988) – "The Lay Members of Christ's Faithful People" – he emphasises the priority of direct proclamation:

The good news is directed to stirring a person to a conversion of heart and life and a clinging to Jesus Christ as Lord and Saviour, to disposing a person to receive Baptism and the Eucharist and to strengthen a person in the prospect and realisation of new life according to the Spirit.' (Christifideles Laici, 33)

The process of evangelisation

1. Pope John Paul II
• "In Christ, God calls all peoples to himself and he wishes to share with them the fullness of his revelation and love" (*Redemptoris Missio*, 55)
• The Gospel must be
  • proclaimed
  • allowed to engage with culture
  • allowed to accompany a person's journey from this life to eternal life
• Pope John Paul II believed that there is a distinctive process between proclaiming the Gospel and its permanent effect on someone's life

2. Pope Benedict XVI

Pope Benedict XVI continued to speak of and to renew the Church's call to the new evangelisation. During his homily on the Solemnity of Saints Peter and Paul at the Basilica of St Paul Outside the Walls on 28 June 2010, he called for a "re-proposing of the Gospel to those regions still awaiting a first evangelisation," and to those regions where the roots of Christianity are deep but have experienced a "serious crisis" of faith due to secularisation.

In talking and writing about the new evangelisation, Pope Benedict constantly explained that it was new:
- not in content, but in its inner thrust
- in its methods that must correspond to the times
- because the Gospel must be re-proclaimed to those who have already heard it

He encouraged the Church to enter into dialogue with modern culture. The Gospel and the Church must confront the cultural crisis brought on by the world's increasing secularisation.

The unchanging mission of the Church is to proclaim the Gospel message to the four corners of the world. The current cultural context and society, however, offer new challenges to the Church, especially in view of declining numbers.

Pontifical Council for the Promotion of the New Evangelisation

Established by Pope Benedict XVI on 21 September 2010, the work of the Pontifical Council for the Promotion of the New Evangelisation is to help the Church to proclaim the Gospel message to an increasingly secular society.

In order to help the new pontifical council to be effective and relevant, Benedict announced that the 2012 Synod of Bishops in Rome would focus on the New Evangelisation.

The 2012 Synod on "The New Evangelisation for the Transmission of the Christian Faith"

On 7 October 2012, three hundred cardinals and bishops gathered in Rome for the Synod on the New Evangelisation for the Transmission of the Christian Faith. They were joined by observers and experts from both the Catholic and non-Catholic worlds.

A Synod in the Catholic Church

- is a non-legislative advisory group, convoked by the Pope, who sets it's theme and agenda and presides over its discussions
- is composed of bishops from across the world
- is permanent, even when not in session
- meets at regular intervals to discuss a theme of particular current importance
- is a forum for practical recommendations for the future activity of the global Church

Called by Pope Benedict XVI before his resignation from the papacy in February 2013, this particular Synod is a landmark in his legacy.

A Church Synod allows a worldwide conversation on a specific topic. That of 2012 concentrated on how to equip Catholics to play their part in the new evangelisation. The bishops hoped to create a new enthusiasm and vitality in the Church's work of spreading the Gospel message of love.

Cares for its members

Celebrates the sacraments

Offers education and guidance in the faith

Engages with those who are searching

Shares its faith

Reaches out beyond parish boundaries

Listens to people

Continually builds community

This Synod gave the Church a dramatically new pastoral approach in its stress on the connections between Jesus and those who believe in him. It challenged us to find innovative ways and methods, as individuals and as communities, of expressing and sharing our faith.

Parish implications of the Synod

Of particular interest to us in this book are the implications of the Synod and the new evangelisation for our parishes. The Synod's preparatory documents and discussions presented us with a very active image of the parish.

The parish is a place where the usual tasks of caring for the active members of the Church takes place: the ordinary day-to-day parish life, catechesis, and the celebration of the sacraments. But the Synod also reminded us that the active parish is to be a centre for sharing faith, listening to people, engaging with those who are searching, and the starting point for sharing God's word and love beyond parish boundaries.

All are welcome!

Several years ago, two pupils on their way to high school decided to play around with an aerosol can and a lighter! Unfortunately they decided to experiment on one of the trees in the grounds of our church. Fortunately for us a local authority street-cleaning van was just passing by and used the water on board to dowse the flames. Sadly, they couldn't save the tree. Unfortunately for the boys, they had school blazers on, and a neighbour also knew the name of one of them. The high school, the police and their parents were then involved.

Their parents wanted them to make some kind of reparation to the church, and so they arranged that the boys would have to save up their pocket money and pay for a new tree. We suggested that they could actually come along to our next maintenance day and help to dig up the charred remains of the tree and plant the new one. We assured them that no one would know why they were there. They turned up for the maintenance day and after they had done their act of reparation, they stayed on (perhaps the free lunch from the fish-and-chip shop was an incentive also!) When they heard that we were having a parish barbecue after the Sunday Mass, they asked if they could come along. Neither of the boys was Catholic, but they arrived in time for Mass, stayed for the whole of it, and joined in the barbecue, chatting with other parishioners they had met the day before. For quite some time after this episode the two boys, when riding their bikes past church, would call in to have a chat with Fr Paul.

What they had done was serious, but it worked out very well: rather than experiencing wrath, they experienced welcome. We would like to think that not using aerosol cans and lighters together wasn't the only lesson that they learnt.

The final message from the bishops present at the Synod for the New Evangelisation began with the image of the woman at the well from St John's Gospel:

"Like Jesus at the well of Sychar, the Church also feels the need to sit beside today's men and women. She wants to render the Lord present in their lives so that they can encounter him because his Spirit alone is the water that gives true and eternal life."
(Message from the Synod on the New Evangelisation, 1)

In sitting beside people we are called to be a welcoming community giving outcasts a home and celebrating and demonstrating the beauty of faith in our Sunday Mass.

Pastoral themes from the Synod

In the closing homily of the Synod, on 28 October 2012, Pope Benedict developed three pastoral themes which he felt emerged from the Synod discussions. They can be summarised as follows:

1. The sacraments of Christian initiation and the appropriate catechesis for their reception will support people as they encounter the Lord's call to holiness – a call addressed to all Christians.

2. The Church's task is to evangelise, to proclaim the message of salvation to those who do not yet know Jesus Christ. We need to pray for the Holy Spirit to arouse a new missionary dynamism in the Church, involving all our people.

3. The baptised who do not live as followers of Christ should be a particular concern, so that they can encounter Jesus Christ anew, rediscover the joy of faith and return to the practice of the faith in the community of their local church.

Pope Benedict referred to the need for new and creative methods of evangelisation, without losing the "tried and true" methods that have been used through the centuries. He encouraged novelty in our approach to bring the Gospel to people today, particularly to those who have grown "tired of the faith". The Synod and Pope Benedict called us back to our roots, to our basic relationship with Jesus Christ and to our need for a vision of hope.

In the following chapters, we will look at some new methods and "novel" ways of bringing the Gospel to people today.

CHAPTER THREE

Pope Francis, *Evangelii Gaudium* and the parish response

Evangelii Gaudium

In an interview with Eugenio Scalfari, the atheist founder of the Italian newspaper, *La Repubblica*, Pope Francis expressed something deep within human hearts when he declared: "We need to get to know each other, listen to each other and improve our knowledge of the world around us." He showed that evangelisation is not about a point-by-point exposition of Church doctrine; instead, it is about opening our eyes and hearts to the people around us. It is about becoming a little more human, a little more loving and a little more understanding as we try to follow Jesus. It is about spreading the joy of the Gospel in our families, homes, parishes and the world around us.

Pope Francis would reflect deeper on this theme. On the 24 November 2013, he issued his Apostolic Exhortation *Evangelii Gaudium – The Joy of the Gospel*. The document is partly in response to the final message and propositions of the 2012 Synod on the New Evangelisation, but it also provides the opportunity for Pope Francis to draw together some of the key messages of the first nine months of his pontificate. The exhortation has been greeted enthusiastically, and is already being seen as a blueprint, a mission statement or mandate for the Church now and well into the future.

This Exhortation and Pope Francis' pontificate to date have generated a new enthusiasm in the Church and for the Church, and his words and witness are proving to be inspirational for many people. While the tone and content of the document are different to the papal documents of his predecessors, its missionary thrust contains a vitally important challenge to the Church as a whole, to local parish communities and to individual Catholics.

The joy of the Gospel in our parish

Pope Francis opens *Evangelii Gaudium* with a note of celebration:

The joy of the Gospel fills the hearts and lives of all who encounter Jesus. Those who accept his offer of salvation are set free from sin, sorrow, inner emptiness and loneliness. With Christ joy is constantly born anew. In this Exhortation I wish to encourage the Christian faithful to embark upon a new chapter of evangelisation marked by this joy, while pointing out new paths for the Church's journey in years to come. (EG, 1)

What is this "new chapter" to which he refers? Well, our best guess would be indicated in the quotation below which seems to sum up the document well:

I dream of a "missionary option", that is, a missionary impulse capable of transforming everything, so that the Church's customs, ways of doing things, times and schedules, language and structures can be suitably channelled for the evangelisation of today's world rather than for her self-preservation. (EG, 27)

This is a bold statement. As a Church, perhaps we have been in self-preservation mode for too long. Pope Francis is calling for our Church to thrive by choosing the missionary option in everything we do.

How do we do this? Well, that's what the rest of *Evangelii Gaudium* is all about.

The following is offered as a way for parishes, groups of parishioners or individuals to reflect on specific aspects of Pope Francis' document, using passages that illustrate some of the major themes. They may help us to evaluate some of our current parish practices and explore possible new practices in our parish communities.

Some major themes in Evangelii Gaudium

The document has several major themes. Below are what we feel are some of the most significant. Many of these themes are emphasised multiple times and in various ways throughout the document. They are:

- the basic proclamation of the Gospel
- we can evangelise only because God first loved us
- our ability to accept the Gospel into our lives
- missionary discipleship
- the parish
- those who are poor

The basic proclamation of the Gospel

For Pope Francis, evangelisation begins by sharing the basic message of the Gospel. He puts the role of those who catechise (and he includes himself in this) at the very heart of the parish. If the catechist does not proclaim the meaning of God's love, then the rest of us are missing out on the heart of the Gospel:

On the lips of the catechist the first proclamation must ring out over and over: "Jesus Christ loves you; he gave his life to save you; and now he is living at your side every day to enlighten, strengthen and free you." (EG, 164)

He goes on to note the importance of the *kerygma* (the basic proclamation of the Gospel) throughout the life of a Christian:

It is… the principal proclamation, the one which we must hear again and again in different ways, the one which we must announce one way or another throughout the process of catechesis, at every level and moment. (EG, 164)

He also practises what he preaches when in the third paragraph he states:

I invite all Christians, everywhere, at this very moment, to a renewed personal encounter with Jesus Christ, or at least an openness to letting him encounter them; I ask all of you to do this unfailingly each day. No one should think that this invitation is not meant for him or her, since "no one is excluded from the joy brought by the Lord". (EG, 3)

Discussion Questions

1. What opportunities does our parish have to share the Gospel message that God loves us?
2. Do we make the most of these opportunities?
3. How can our parish help people to meet Jesus?

"Every baptised member of the Catholic faith is called to evangelise and be a missionary disciple."

We can evangelise only because God first loved us.
An evangelising community knows that the Lord has taken the initiative. He has loved us first (see 1 John 4:19). Therefore we can move forward, boldly take the initiative, go out to others, seek those who have fallen away, stand at the crossroads and welcome those who feel lost or excluded.

Our evangelisation depends on the earlier theme: our willingness to welcome the Lord who first loved us.

Here we find the source and inspiration of all our efforts at evangelisation. For if we have received the love which restores meaning to our lives, how can we fail to share that love with others? (EG, 8)

Discussion Questions

1. How do we ensure that our parishes are places that encourage and train people to be evangelisers?
2. How do we create our parishes as centres of constant missionary outreach?

Missionary disciple

The term "missionary disciple" is used throughout *Evangelii Gaudium*. The two words hold in tension both the need for a relationship with our Lord and the need to go to the margins of society to preach the Gospel. One thing is very clear in Pope Francis' document – every baptised member of the Catholic faith is called to evangelise and be a missionary disciple:

In virtue of their baptism, all the members of the People of God have become missionary disciples (see Matthew 28:19). All the baptised, whatever their position in the Church or their level of instruction in the faith, are agents of evangelisation. (EG, 120)

What I would like to propose is something much more in the line of an evangelical discernment. It is the approach of a missionary disciple, an approach "nourished by the light and strength of the Holy Spirit". (EG, 50)

The Church is herself a missionary disciple. (EG, 40)

Discussion Questions

1. How can we convince people that they have what it takes to be extremely effective missionary disciples?
2. What support and encouragement can we offer them?
3. How can we help each other to move beyond our comfort zones as we reach out to others?
4. As a parish, are we ready to take the message of God's love to those who are living on the margins of society?
5. How can we do this?

The parish

Pope Francis spends a considerable amount of time on the parish as he looks to see how a missionary impulse would change parish life:

In all its activities the parish encourages and trains its members to be evangelisers. It is a community of communities, a sanctuary where the thirsty come to drink in the midst of their journey, and a centre of constant missionary outreach. We must admit, though, that the call to review and renew our parishes has not yet sufficed to bring them nearer to people, to make them environments of living communion and participation, and to make them completely mission-oriented. (EG, 28)

In some people we see an ostentatious preoccupation for the liturgy, for doctrine and for the Church's prestige, but without any concern that the Gospel have a real impact on God's faithful people and the concrete needs of the present time. (EG, 95)

Then in regards to sharing the message of the Gospel:

Pastoral ministry in a missionary style is not obsessed with the disjointed transmission of a multitude of doctrines to be insistently imposed… the message has to concentrate on the essentials, on what is most beautiful, most grand, most appealing and at the same time most necessary. The message is simplified, while losing none of its depth and truth, and thus becomes all the more forceful and convincing. (EG, 35)

Those who are poor

Since the beginning of his pontificate, Pope Francis has expressed his desire for, "a Church which is poor and for the poor." The place of poor people occupies a significant section in his *Exhortation* and his words deserve to be closely examined by individuals and parish communities.

The following are some significant quotes to help sum up his thoughts:

We know that, "evangelisation would not be complete if it did not take account of the unceasing interplay of the Gospel and of man's concrete life, both personal and social". (EG, 181)

Each individual Christian and every community is called to be an instrument of God for the liberation and promotion of the poor, and for enabling them to be fully a part of society. (EG, 187)

Inspired by this, the Church has made an option for the poor which is understood as a, "'special form of primacy in the exercise of Christian charity, to which the whole tradition of the Church bears witness". (EG, 198)

God's heart has a special place for the poor, so much so that he himself "became poor" (2 Cor 8:9). The entire history of our redemption is marked by the presence of the poor. Salvation came to us from the "yes" uttered by a lowly maiden from a small town on the fringes of a great empire. (EG, 197)

Without the preferential option for the poor, "the proclamation of the Gospel, which is itself the prime form of charity, risks being misunderstood or submerged by the ocean of words which daily engulfs us in today's society of mass communications". (EG, 199)

Pope Francis thinks that the Church should pay more attention to the needs of poor people, those who are marginalised and people who have suffered injustice. He has set us a challenge – how will we respond as individuals and as a parish community?

*E*veryone can teach us a lesson. As a parish we are very aware of the value that people with disabilities bring to the parish community. One such person was Colin who at 33 years old was very severely handicapped and suffered from Cerebral Palsy. Although he only lives ten minutes' walk from the church, he was one of the first parishioners to take advantage of our Sunday morning minibus pickup. He came, with his carer, to the 10.30am Mass every Sunday. At first we worried how Colin would negotiate getting up and down the two steps of the minibus, but Colin wasn't going to let his limited mobility stop him from having the Sunday morning ride to church. He soon worked out that getting up the steps was fine with help from the driver and helper; it didn't take long for him to work out that if he slid off the seat and slid down the steps on his back, he could be out quicker than our more elderly passengers.

Colin had no speech and just walked around church all through Mass, but somehow never went into the sanctuary area during Mass. He loved babies and would stop and look adoringly at any that he came across in church; he also liked women with blond hair, who would receive the same adoring look! He was a very important member of our parish community, so much so that if ever he missed an appearance at Mass people made a point of enquiring about him before leaving Church to go home. When he died suddenly in 2010, there was a real sense of shock and bereavement among the 10.30am congregation.

When it came to his funeral the church was full and he is still remembered with affection today.

People with disabilities bring something really positive to a parish. Our young people especially benefit from being exposed to others whom many would see as being "less fortunate than themselves". Colin taught them they do not need to have any worries or inhibitions when it comes to communicating with people who have disabilities.

CHAPTER FOUR

Whom do we evangelise and when do we evangelise?

The starting place of evangelisation

One of Pope Francis' first interviews was with the Jesuit *America* magazine. Here, a comment he made about the future direction of the Church was also a remark about the changes he would find necessary in his own life:

Instead of being just a Church that welcomes and receives by keeping the doors open, let us try also to be a Church that finds new roads, that is able to step outside itself and go to those who do not attend Mass, to those who have quit or are indifferent.

Perhaps, then, it might be worthwhile to listen to another observation he made within the same 2013 interview. Within a single sentence, Pope Francis laid down a template for evangelisation:

I see clearly that the thing the Church needs most today is the ability to heal wounds and to warm the hearts of the faithful; it needs nearness, proximity.

In other words, evangelisation brings God into the reality of people's often messy lives in a way that is warm, human, compassionate and Christ-like.

Beginning from here and now

As Christians and especially as Catholics, like the disciples we are commanded by Jesus to, "go and make disciples of all nations, baptising them in the name of the Father and of the Son and of the Holy Spirit." (Matthew 28:19) Peter says to all Christians, "Be prepared to give an answer to everyone who asks you to give the reason for the hope that you have." (1 Peter 3:15). Peter says this to explain how we are to, "set apart Christ as Lord," that is, how we are to obey him. We should evangelise because God commands it.

God's love should compel us to show compassion to all those in need. Consider how richly God has loved us (1 John 3:1; 4:10). If we are to love our neighbour as ourselves (Matthew 7:12), we should love them as we have been loved, which, at the very least, means sharing the Gospel with them.

Ultimately, our motivation to evangelise, to spread the Good News of Jesus Christ, is the glorification of God; this is brought about only when the truth about God is known and made known.

Often, when people think of the new evangelisation, they imagine people going off to convert pagans in foreign countries, when, really, in this day and age, we need to look closer to home. Blessed Mother Teresa once said, "The way you help to heal the world is to start with your own family."

Some Catholics, for whatever reason, no longer feel part of the Church. As Catholics and as one family in the Church, we too need to "start at home". We must somehow let these people know that there *is* a place for them; that our parish is waiting and longing, with open hearts and arms, to welcome them home.

In our diocesan outreach, we spend time working within the prison system with young men who, in some cases, through no fault of their own, have become caught up in a life they felt unable to leave behind.

Those prisoners who call themselves Catholic, often feel that they no longer have a place in the Church and that the Church does not want them. Not only has society rejected them; they feel that the Church has too.

We spend time helping the prisoners to look at ways of bringing God back into their lives. We try to help them to understand that Jesus was born into the chaos and confusion of this world, not into a tidy and perfect realm. God chose to send down his Son into a borrowed stable, cradled in far from perfect surroundings. The first people to visit Jesus were the shepherds – men who were considered beggars and thieves in the society of their time.

God is in the mess of all our lives

During another six-week Lenten programme we gave in the same prison, we were astonished by the knowledge that certain prisoners had about the Bible, some even being able to quote relevant chapter and verse at the drop of a hat. One young man, perhaps no more than twenty, but not a stranger to institutional living, having spent time in young offenders institutes from a young age, listened intently whilst his fellow inmates explained their understanding of what they had heard. From what they had seen in the films clips we had shown, they made comparisons to Jesus' life. Then quite openly the twenty-year old said, "You know this Jesus guy? The only time I ever hear about him is when I'm in prison." If that is the case, then we thank God for our prison chaplaincies.

Addressing the needs of a prison population is a unique situation. Yet it is one that encourages us to bring Jesus' message into the ordinariness of everyday life. The following quote from *Evangelii Gaudium* encourages us to move forward:

Ordinary pastoral ministry seeks to help believers to grow spiritually so that they can respond to God's love ever more fully in their lives…
[But] we cannot forget that evangelisation is first and foremost about preaching the Gospel to those who do not know Jesus Christ or who have always rejected him… All of them have a right to receive the Gospel. Christians have the duty to proclaim the Gospel without excluding anyone. Instead of seeming to impose new obligations, they should appear as people who wish to share their joy… It is not by proselytizing that the Church grows, but "by attraction". (EG, 15)

How do you think we can do this? In everyday parish life we are presented with opportunities to evangelise and it is up to us to recognise that we do so primarily through our own witness. The following are a few opportunities for telling others of the wonder of God's love.

Let your light shine

Several years ago, we invited parishioners during Lent to pray for someone they know who might love returning to a regular practice of their faith (something we do every Lent and Advent). One of our parishioners shared with us the story of what happened. She lit a candle on our special Lenten candle stand, and she prayed each day for her husband who had not been to church for many years. She also knew that what she had done so far was the easy part, lighting a candle and praying; the hardest part was yet to come and that was to invite her husband to come to church with her.

*"All of them
have a right to
receive the Gospel.
Christians have the
duty to proclaim
the Gospel without
excluding anyone."*

On Holy Saturday evening, just before she was leaving for the Easter Vigil she shouted up the stairs to her husband that she was going to the Easter Vigil in a few minutes. She then added, "Do you want to come with me?" To her amazement her husband shouted back, "Yes, just give me a couple of minutes and I'll be with you." He came back to church to the most beautiful and powerful liturgy of the Church's year, and the longest liturgy of the year also! But it didn't put him off, he's still here, and now very much involved in the life of the parish. His wife's prayers, example, witness and faith had brought him back to the church.

Baptism

Why do parents come to your parish and ask for their baby to be baptised? For sure, some will make their request because they are practising Catholics who want to bring up their child within a faith-filled family. Other parents, who are not Catholic or not religious, will have a variety of motives.

Some parents might, for instance, be looking ahead to an easier future enrolment in a Catholic school. Others might simply consider baptism the official naming ceremony for their little one without looking more deeply into the significance of the event. Perhaps non-practising Catholic parents still feel that they want their child "done" and then they can feel they have done their duty.

And the godparents? Are they chosen because they will take an active interest in the life and faith development of their godchild? Are they friends, perhaps with no faith commitment, who will be good for birthday and Christmas presents?

Pope Francis suggests that baptism is a unique opportunity for evangelisation for "the baptized whose lives do not reflect the demands of Baptism", who lack a meaningful relationship to the Church and no longer experience the consolation born of faith.

He points out that, "The Church, in her maternal concern, tries to help them experience a conversion which will restore the joy of faith to their hearts and inspire a commitment to the Gospel." (*EG*, 15)

During the celebration of baptism, after establishing the name that parents wish to give to their child, the first words asked of them are, "What do you ask of God's Church for your child?" The simple answer is, "Baptism."

At this point we, as a parish, have a great opportunity to help these parents to recognise that they are offering their child the promise of eternal life through Jesus Christ. Through a well thought-out baptismal programme we can open up a new life not only for their baby but for them too! By taking time to help them to understand what they may see as being "in their past", we can offer them through their child's baptism, the chance to take a fresh look at their own faith.

Here are a few suggestions which may encourage parents to look again at their faith.

1. Ask them to bring their own baptismal certificate to a baptism preparation meeting.
(*This enables them to take a look at where their journey of faith began.*)
2. Ask them to make sure that at least one godparent is a practising Catholic.
(*This reinforces the importance of continuity in the child's faith life.*)
3. In order to highlight the importance of the support of the parish community, welcome the child during a Sunday Mass, using the opening words of the baptism service.

4. Invite all of the children baptised in the previous year to join the parish community for a special Mass on or around the Feast of the Baptism of the Lord. (*This also gives another opportunity to welcome the parents back to church again and confirms their place in the parish community.*)

Many parents experience a rebirth in themselves as they see their future through the lives of their new-born child. In welcoming them as part of the parish, they have the opportunity to see and appreciate the great gift that they received at their own baptism.

"Many parents experience a rebirth in themselves as they see their future through the lives of their new-born child."

Sacramental preparation
Do you remember the day of your First Holy Communion? What about confirmation? Did you receive that sacrament shortly after your First Holy Communion, or did you wait a few years until you were older?

For Catholic children in the setting of a Catholic school, the preparation and celebration of both these sacraments will be major landmarks. They are also a positive experience of what it means to be an active member of a community of faith.

For those who do not attend a Catholic school, the parish must take the responsibility of teaching its candidates the importance of the sacraments in their daily life.

A child who understands the meaning and significance of the sacraments is more likely to value them as an ongoing part of daily life.

In our diocese our seven-year-olds undertake a "Sacramental Programme". This means that they spend the whole of Year Three preparing for their confirmation, their

A parents' meeting is not simply an information session on what their children will be doing. Rather, with the aid of other material, we encourage them to look again at their impressions of the Church. Such a group usually consists of twenty percent churchgoing parents; the remaining eighty percent are a mixture of those who do not go to Mass and those who feel rejected by a Church which they feel is irrelevant.

Towards the end of the programme, we bring the families (including brothers and sisters) together for a full–day retreat. This gives them the opportunity to reflect on the step which the child is about to make, while also enjoying a day of family togetherness.

We bring young people who have recognised the importance of having Jesus in their lives to share their talents and talk about the impact in their life of having Jesus as their friend and guide.

One outcome of these days is that some parents discover a renewed interest in their faith as a result of sharing a momentous milestone in the lives of their child.

Marriage

These days it seems that marriage preparation for most people means arranging for dresses and outfits, for flowers, for cars, for seating plans and for favours. For couples marrying in church, however, there is another dimension to their wedding: in front of their family and friends but, more importantly, in the sight of God, they give themselves to each other, "for better, for worse, for richer for poorer, in sickness and in health, to love and to cherish, till death do us part."

Increasingly, couples coming to church to be married include of one partner who is not a Catholic and who might be non-baptised or an unbeliever. Some of these

First Holy Communion and for their first celebration of the sacrament of reconciliation. (Diocesan practices vary regarding confirmation.)

This is a perfect environment for evangelisation, not only for the children, but also for their parents and grandparents. Many adult relatives report that the child's sacramental preparation gives them the opportunity to revisit their own faith life.

With this in mind, we feel that preparing parents separately from their children means that we can give them a more grown-up experience. For their part, the children experience something more meaningful to their particular age and interests.

while many would admit that they have no interest in the Church.

Whatever the reason for choosing to have a Catholic marriage ceremony, it is an opportunity for evangelisation.

Preparation for marriage can be quite intense and some partners will find that this exposure to Catholicism kindles some interest in finding out more about the Church.

Encourage them to come along to your parish RCIA or Journey of Faith groups just to find out more about the Church. This will give both of them a deeper understanding of Catholicism. Sometimes this informal encouragement results in the non-Catholic partner taking steps towards becoming a Catholic.

If the only outcome, however, is a greater understanding of his or her partner's faith, then greater harmony is achieved.

Funerals

If you were to ask the majority of priests what brings more people back to a practice of the faith, they would say, "a bereavement". At a time of loss most people bring a personal history of a time of grief, along with their own history of faith or lack of faith.

No matter how disconnected from the Church and religion, grief is an evangelisation opportunity. The message of eternal life engenders the hope of seeing loved ones again in the fullness of God's kingdom.

might recognise the importance of and the commitment involved in getting married in the Catholic Church, whereas others might not.

To most, the reason for marrying in the Catholic Church is out of respect and love for their Catholic partners

We live in a world where belief in the afterlife has diminished. So, as Christians, and especially as Catholics, our message must be that, "life is changed: it is not ended." We pray that the deceased may enter God's welcoming embrace. We ask that God give hope to those loved ones left behind. It is often this inherent

> *"A funeral must embrace everybody with understanding and compassion."*

belief in life after death that gives us strength to carry on with life.

Our awareness of the promise of eternal life is given to us in St Paul's Letter to the Romans when he asked the question:

Are you unaware that we who were baptised into Christ Jesus were baptised into his death? We were indeed buried with him through baptism into death, so that, just as Christ was raised from the dead by the glory of the Father, we too might live in newness of life. (Romans 6:3-4. 8-9).

Very often when we celebrate a funeral we have with us an "incidental community". The impact of a death goes well beyond our parishes. People are ready and willing to travel long distances for a funeral. Some want it to be a celebration of the life that has just gone and, at the same time, many people present will be searching to understand the meaning of suffering and death. Any funeral party includes relatives and friends from near and far. There will be a mixture of practising and non-practising Catholics. People of other faiths or none who knew the deceased and their families will be present.

A funeral must embrace everybody with understanding and compassion.

Our way of communicating eternal life at the time of a funeral is the message of eternal life, one that relates to our own day. It is healing and hopeful for all those who search for meaning and purpose, especially at this time of sadness. Our message is not about death; rather, it is about life in eternity. It is a proclamation of a new and undying life in the kingdom of God.

Often at times like these, the simplest message has the most impact. Bereavement can be described as "slow burning" – so often it can just catch someone out, weeks and months later, and it will be the support and kindness of the initial welcome at the time of loss that will bring people back to the parish for support.

Our parish Bereavement Support Team contacts the next-of-kin a month or so after the funeral, just to check if they need anything. They will offer practical support, a chat, or a chance to go for coffee. They offer to help with form-filling, and in some cases, where a husband or wife has been the one bringing them to Mass, offer them a place on the parish minibus to bring them to Sunday Mass, or to events in the parish. Where more professional help is needed, they will contact the parish office and the appropriate agencies can be contacted. All these instances open up avenues for evangelisation.

In October each year, we write to all the families of those whose funerals have taken place in our parish since the previous October. In the letter we mention the deceased by name and their relationship to the next of kin. We invite them to join us at our annual Mass for and with the bereaved at a specific parish Mass on one of the Sundays in November.

When the families arrive they are welcomed by members of our bereavement team, who give them a small booklet of prayers and scripture readings which may be of help to them during the time of bereavement. When they enter the church they see A4 laminated colour posters around the church, each with the name of a deceased parishioner on it, simply remembering them and asking people to pray for them.

During the Mass each of the deceased is mentioned by name in the prayers of intercession, (including deceased members of our parishioners families whose funerals took place elsewhere) and at the same time a candle is lit for each of them.

After Mass the families are invited to join us for refreshments in the parish centre, which gives another chance to connect with them.

The posters of each of the deceased are displayed in church throughout the month of November, and each weekend at all the Masses parishioners are invited to look at the poster, find the name of someone they don't know, and pray for that person during the coming week. The following Sunday they are invited to do the same again for someone else.

At the end of November, we again write to the families, sending them the laminated poster (which many people have already asked for at the Mass for the bereaved) along with another copy of the prayers for a time of bereavement. We also include a sheet entitled *Coping with Bereavement in December,* designed to help people get through the first Christmas without their loved one.

The annual Mass with and for the bereaved has been the catalyst for many people to return to a regular practice of their faith: they see that the parish has not forgotten them after the funeral. Relatives tell us that they appreciate the on-going pastoral care the parish offers.

Schools

With two primary schools in our parish we make materials available so that non-Catholic parents can be fully aware of what is available to assist them in understanding life in a Catholic family. Offering opportunities for them to join our "Seeking Christ" group, allows them to ask the questions which they had always wanted to pose but had never previously had the opportunity. Sometimes this approach even leads them to becoming Catholics themselves.

Welcome Sunday

In our parish, on the First Sunday of Advent, we invite those parishioners who are new to the parish to join other parishioners for breakfast in our parish centre. What better opportunity to welcome new friends than to eat together? During this time we encourage them to introduce themselves or allow someone to introduce them, so that everyone knows who they are and make them welcome. Our motto for this day is: *"A stranger is a friend that you have not yet met."*

In our parish and in yours there will be family members who have been away from the regular practice of the faith for many years. Each will have their own story to tell of why they left; it is our job to bring them back in to the fold. To assist them in breaking down these barriers we have a programme which is called, *"While you were away"*. This programme takes a look at how the Church has changed over the years, especially since Vatican II.

"A stranger is a friend that you have not yet met."

Through the medium of film, we take them back in time to look at the Church pre-Vatican II and then post-Vatican II. In doing this we explore Dan Rivers' theory in his book *From Maintenance to Mission* of a Church going through a time of Orientation (pre-Vatican II), then Disorientation (Implementation of Vatican II) and then Re-orientation (post-Vatican II). Most people discover a very different Church from the one they left behind.

The Welcome and Information Centre

Recently we established our Welcome and Information Centre just off the main body of the church. It's a place where a team of trained parishioners are always available after the weekend Masses to provide information to fellow parishioners and especially new members of the parish. It also contains contact information for local organisations such as "Christians Against Poverty", our local Caritas centre and others.

The Welcome Pack

This pack, which includes a letter of welcome from the parish priest, is sent out to every new parishioner. Inside are details of everything that goes on in the parish, with contact information of everyone involved in the various groups and ministries, together with parish office contact numbers and e-mail addresses. This includes information on our schools and also informs them about what the parish offers regarding baptisms, marriages and funerals.

The contact details of the new arrivals are put on our database. They will then automatically receive information about parish events.

The weekly newsletter is available online on the parish website or e-mailed weekly to those who want it.

Finally, on reflection, if asked, "To whom do we evangelise and when do we evangelise?" – the answer must be that we see everyone we meet as being open to evangelisation. Every occasion is an evangelising opportunity.

CHAPTER FIVE

Let's get started!

"The important thing is not to walk alone, but to rely on each other as brothers and sisters"

Our Parish Audit

As a parish priest working together with all members of our parish community, I and they are called upon to spread the Good News of Jesus Christ. By virtue of our own baptism we all become participants in the work that is the central mission of the church: evangelisation. Most people might think this to mean going out into the street and dragging poor unsuspecting atheists or returning Catholics kicking and screaming into a church that holds little or no significance for them. Certainly, evangelisation does not mean that! In the words of Pope Francis:

I invite everyone to be bold and creative in this task of rethinking the goals, structures, style and methods of evangelisation in their respective communities...The important thing is not to walk alone, but to rely on each other as brothers and sisters. (EG,13)

Before we can take up this challenge of reaching out to others, we have a more difficult task: that of evangelising the evangelised.

Most Catholic parishes are wonderful places where families live and grow in their faith. In such communities, each generation can look with affection and warmth at the parish that gave them the foundation on which to build their faith.

Alternatively, they can look back at an experience of parish to which they would not submit their children. There may be enduring memories of a cold draughty church and an even colder response to their developing faith needs. Unfortunately, the joy of Jesus which Pope Francis describes is not always the experience that we remember.

What a welcome!

When I was at the Catholic Missionary Society, we would occasionally have a Sunday when we weren't out in a parish somewhere in England or Wales either leading a mission or preparing with the parish for a mission. On these occasions I would always go to a local parish for Sunday Mass and join the congregation.

Eventually I started to attend one particular church, and although I wasn't there every Sunday, I was very much aware that after about eight or nine months, no one had ever spoken to me apart from the Sign of Peace. Then one Sunday morning in December, you can imagine my delight as I saw someone making a beeline for me in the church porch – it was obvious they were going to speak to me at last. "Good morning, would you like to buy a raffle ticket for the Christmas draw?" was the greeting I received.

Well, at least someone had spoken to me. I supported the Christmas raffle; I didn't win a prize, but it did make me think about how welcoming we really are as a church.

In this chapter we would like to give you the opportunity to look openly at the kind of environment we provide for our parishioners. However, before we start, we want to stress that the purpose of this exercise is not to criticise or undermine, but to offer a springboard for what is possible for your parish in the future.

This short survey can be used to look candidly at the kind of environment and welcome we provide, not only for the stranger at the door but also for our fellow parishioners.

This is only a suggested point to start: your parish may find alternative ways of working through the survey. That is fine: the end-point is the important part of this exercise. How a parish reaches it depends entirely on its own choices.

We suggest a number of sessions so that time can be given to consider your findings.

1. Gather a group of parishioners – not more than ten. Choose a mixture of ages and abilities. Try to find people who can be honest without being unnecessarily critical.
2. Set aside one evening – perhaps over refreshments – to look at this Parish Audit. Be honest. Give each individual a copy to answer briefly.
3. It may be necessary to take some time to look around the church and its grounds.
4. Appoint one person to collate the answers.

Ideally, at this point, if the parish priest has not been able to join you, then ask him to join you at another meeting so that the group can discuss its findings with him. Again, this should be a positive exercise with an eye to the future, not a sullen review of things that have gone wrong.

Our parish audit

FIRST EVENING

Here are some questions for all of us to consider in assessing how welcoming our parish is to others.

Why we are looking at our parish

This survey has several aims:

- To see what is working well
- To discover what we could do better
- To cater for the needs and diversity of our parishioners
- To come up with new ideas
- To work out whether we should concentrate on what we are already doing or look at new initiatives
- To prepare for future planning

Most parishes are made up of a variety of groups. These are just a few of them:

- Young adults
- Young married couples
- Elderly married couples
- Primary school children
- Teens
- Singles: young to middle-age
- Singles: elderly, living alone
- Widowed
- Single parent families
- Newcomers
- Sick/Housebound/in Nursing Homes
- Divorced/Separated
- Remarried
- Unemployed

First Impressions

- Are the Church grounds neat and tidy?
- Is the entrance clearly marked and brightly lit on dark nights?
- Is there a notice of service times that can be read from outside the church?
- Is the information on the noticeboard up to date?
- Is the information provided in the church porch updated regularly? Are the notices bright and colourful, making them interesting to read?
- Is there plenty of information about parish activities and is it clear where people can find information about forthcoming events?
- Is the car park clearly signposted and is it safe for people at night?
- Does the church sound system work adequately?
- Do we have a loop system for hearing aid users?
- Do we have a sign to inform people of our loop?
- Is the church warm enough or do people have to wear coats to keep warm?
- Are toilet facilities available and easy to locate?
- Do we provide a large print newsletter or service sheet for the visually impaired?
- Are all areas accessible to those using wheelchairs?

The Welcome

- How do we greet people when they come to church?
- Does anyone give out hymn books, Mass books, service sheets?
- Do members of the congregation openly greet or welcome others around them?
- Do parishioners greet and welcome people at baptisms, funerals and other services?
- Are newcomers formally welcomed at the start of a service?
- Do we have some form of Mass/service booklet that indicates to a non-Catholic visitor where to stand or sit during the Mass/service?
- Are people who cannot receive communion invited to come forward for a blessing?
- Do the priest or designated lay people greet people on arrival at the back of the church?

How child-friendly is our church?

- Is there an area where children/toddlers can go so as not to disturb others?
- Do we provide feeding and changing facilities for young children?
- Is there a children's Liturgy of the Word or other specific activity for children?
- Are members of the congregation involved in the children's liturgy?
- Are the children involved in the Procession of the Gifts?
- Are young children encouraged to come for a blessing at communion?
- Do young people generally play an active part in the service?

Following up the welcome

- Do we provide tea/coffee after services? Are newcomers openly invited?
- Are there welcome cards for newcomers to fill in their names and contact details?
- Does the parish have a welcome pack to give or send newcomers?
- How soon are newcomers contacted after their first introduction?
- Does the parish have a process for welcoming "returning" Catholics?
- Does the parish organise events specifically to welcome people?

Catering for everyone's needs

- Do we have parking facilities for the disabled? How easy is it for disabled people to access the church?
- Are people with disabilities invited to undertake liturgical ministries?
- Are all social/ethnic groups included in the life of the parish?
- Does the church have a bookstall or repository or library?
- Are there regular social events in the parish?

Parish Communication

- Does the parish have contact with the local press?
- Does the parish have a website? Is it updated regularly?
- Does the parish post newsletters to those who cannot come to church, or offer an e-mail newsletter to parishioners?

Our parish audit

SECOND EVENING

Here are some questions for us to consider with regard to how your parish supports families. It is not expected that we should offer all that is listed. The important point is that we create a parish community where families feel that they belong, whether they are passing through or staying for many years. Is our parish the kind of environment that actively supports parents/carers/families? Are they given space to develop as Christians themselves, and how much help do they receive as they introduce their faith to their children? Does our parish community help families to feel comfortable and valued?

"Does our parish community help families to feel comfortable and valued?"

- Do we provide baptism preparation? Do non-Catholic partners feel welcome?
- Do we offer practical support to young families?
- Do we have a parent and toddler group which welcomes families from the wider community?
- Do we offer support for children who do not attend Catholic schools?
- How do we cater for non-Catholic partners when children are preparing for the sacraments?
- Is our sacramental preparation programme sensitive to families in different domestic situations or does it assume that all children are living with two parents in a traditional family setting?
- Does everybody know who is responsible in the parish for the protection of children and vulnerable adults?
- What is available for young people in our parish?
- How does our parish link in with young people at secondary school?
- Do young people in our parish participate in any deanery/diocesan activity, such as the Lourdes Group, World Youth Day events and the like?

- Do we have any church services specifically for or focused on young people?
- How do we help parents of young people? Do we run any courses or groups for single, separated or divorced parents? How do we support parents of teenagers?
- Do we have any parish activities where all the family can join in and have fun, such as socials, outings, sports events, weekend breaks and the like?
- Does our liturgy (words and music) reflect our community? Can parishioners participate actively in the celebration?
- Do we have a parish magazine? Is it sent to housebound parishioners?
- Do we provide opportunities for sharing skills, experience and information?
- Do we have a supply of leaflets and information available on life's problem areas?
- Do we know where to find help for families who are looking for support with social issues/problems, such as bullying, drug/alcohol abuse, domestic violence and so on?

After due consideration of the Parish Audit, it is time to look at an Action Plan

CREATING AN ACTION PLAN FOR OUR PARISH

After thinking about the results of our survey, it is time to look at an Action Plan. This can help our parish to support its established members, and to move forward in welcoming and helping to engage new and returning Catholics.

Parish name:

Key aspects of our Parish Welcome that we want to share and celebrate are:

Short-term actions that we will take to develop the Ministry of Welcome in our parish are:

Obstacles/barriers we have identified in developing our Parish Welcome are:

A few areas for possible consideration in our Action Plan are the following:

The parish will provide for faith development through the following:

- Parish renewal programmes
- Retreats
- Scripture study
- Liturgy of the Word for children
- Youth programmes
- Faith sharing groups
- Devotional opportunities

The parish sees the Eucharist as central to parish life. We will foster its development in the following ways:

- Greeting and welcome
- Prayer-filled liturgy and active participation
- Ensuring that communal worship is accessible to all
- Providing opportunity for people to meet together after Mass

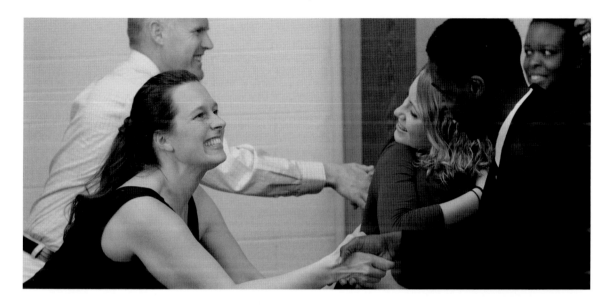

Parishioners will be involved in sacramental celebrations by:

Our parish will reach out to the wider community in the following ways:

We will train parishioners to listen and offer a sincere welcome to those who are:
- Returning to the Catholic Church after an absence
- Divorced and separated
- Remarried
- Hurting
- Hungry
- Feeling alone or isolated in the community
- Stressed
- Emotionally burdened
- Victims of violence

List any other ways in which our parish can evangelise.

CHAPTER SIX

Parish evangelisation teams

The 1983 *Code of Canon Law* states that it is a requirement that all parishes have a finance committee:

In each parish there is to be a finance council which is governed, in addition to universal law, by norms issued by the diocesan bishop and in which the Christian faithful, selected according to these same norms, are to assist the pastor in the administration of the goods of the parish, without prejudice to the prescript of canon 532. (Code of Canon Law, 537)

Perhaps many parishes do have something resembling a finance council. The *Code* also states that:

If the diocesan bishop judges it opportune after he has heard the presbyteral council, a pastoral council is to be established in each parish, over which the pastor presides and in which the Christian faithful, together with those who share in pastoral care by virtue of their office in the parish, assist in fostering pastoral activity. (Code of Canon Law, 536)

Perhaps there are more pastoral councils than finance councils. Is it surprising that there is no mention in the *Code of Canon Law* of a requirement for a parish to have a specific group of people who are responsible for evangelisation in a parish?

As we explore the possibilities of establishing and forming a parish evangelisation team in this chapter, we will see that there is a downside and an upside to setting up an evangelisation team. To give such a group in a parish canonical status could, in fact, cause some problems.

The Year of Faith (2012-2013), called by Pope Benedict XVI, ended during the pontificate of Pope Francis. It provided the Church with a valuable opportunity for our parishioners to consider and grow in their faith. The Year of Faith encouraged people to feel more confident about sharing their religious beliefs with others.

A fruitful legacy of the Year of Faith in our parishes could be the formation of parish evangelisation teams.

How to go about setting up a parish evangelisation team

- Invite eight to ten people from the parish – those who have either expressed an interest in evangelisation or whom you feel would make good members of the team – to come together and meet with the parish clergy
- At the introductory meeting, outline a programme of formation for the team, which will involve reflection on the Church in the modern world and evangelisation

The team can then begin to meet together for a time of formation and prayer.

- At the end of the time of formation the parish priest could commission the parish evangelisation team in the presence of the parish community on a given Sunday. In commissioning the team, the parish priest will have an opportunity to explain what exactly its role is and its responsibilities to the whole parish

- After the commissioning, the new team will need to be supported in their ministry by the parish priest. The team will need to engage regularly in the work of finding new resources for themselves and for the people in their parish

The downside for a parish evangelisation team

There will be a downside if the new members do not undergo a time of formation and reflection. Unless there is proper formation and reflection, they may feel that they are the only ones in the parish who have to do the evangelising (hence the danger of giving them canonical status as mentioned above). They can also burn-out easily if they have unreal expectations of themselves or if others have unreal expectations of them. Any evangelisation work will fail without prayerful reflection and openness to the guidance of the Holy Spirit.

The upside for a parish evangelisation team

There will surely be a great benefit to the parish when the team members share a positive outlook, benefit from good formation, have patience with the project and trust in each other. They can help a parish community and the individuals in the community to adapt their thinking so that more parishioners are able to see how they are called to be evangelisers and how they can become involved in the mission of the Church. The team can really help a parish see more clearly how most parish programmes and parish events are opportunities for evangelisation, and they can play their part in helping their parish move from being a good welcoming parish into an excellent witnessing parish.

Parish evangelisation teams

Whom should you consider inviting to be on the team?

- Committed Catholics
- People who are open to new ways of doing things
- People who have experience with the unchurched or lapsed Catholics
- People who are able to work with people who have doubts
- People who are non-judgemental and flexible
- People who are not overly committed already
- Male and female, with a good mixture of age-ranges

How to select people to be part of the team

- Invite people personally: if you extend a general invitation, you will likely end up with the wrong people
- Avoid asking those who are already over-burdened
- Seek out those you feel are open to new experiences of God through others
- Seek out those you feel will be good at working as part of a team
- Seek out those who have shown an interest, for example in *Evangelii Gaudium*, as this is going to be the blueprint for mission and evangelisation for many years to come

What will they do during the time of formation?

This will be the time when they will be invited to become familiar with some of the basic Church texts relating to evangelisation, especially in the context of the parish. Over a series of meetings they will have the opportunity to look at the Gospel mandate for mission and its implications, and then move forward to some of the key ideas, from Paul VI's encyclical *Evangelii Nuntiandi* (1975), leading to a fuller appreciation of Pope Francis' *Evangelii Gaudium*.

After this they will explore a simple review of the parish in terms of evangelisation; they will look at where the parish is now, what needs to change, what can be improved; they will evaluate the parish's strengths and weaknesses, and how evangelisation is seen in the parish; they will find out which individuals or groups are actively and consciously involved in evangelisation. They will finish their time of formation reflecting on what it means to be the Church in a secular society.

The purpose of the time of formation

- Firstly, to form a group of people into a team who can work together and draw on their different strengths, skills and talents
- To form a team who have a basic understanding of the call to evangelisation and its priority in the life of the Church
- To begin the process of identifying the work that lies ahead in making the whole parish community more missionary and conscious of being part of the Church's mission
- To begin to identify what is already happening, and promote new opportunities and methods for being an inviting and evangelising parish

Important principles for the parish evangelisation team

- Members must pace themselves – not try to run before they have learned to walk, and be careful to avoid burn-out through trying to do too much too quickly
- Resist the temptation to just 'get on with it' without using the time of formation and the time for prayerful preparation
- Members must be realistic in setting their goals at the end of the formation period, remembering that it is God's Church and that we are God's servants
- Members must learn to utilise, encourage and resource existing groups, ministries and individuals
- Members must remain connected to and in communication with the parish clergy and the whole parish community
- Hopefully members will see that they are to be, in a very gentle way, the evangelising conscience of the parish, constantly asking this question about all parish activity: "What does this have to do with evangelisation?" This will lead to a new way of being a parish and a new way of using our parish resources

A suggested programme of formation

This is not exhaustive, and various different elements can be added according to each parish situation. What we present here is an outline, using various chapters in this book as a resource for formation.

First formation meeting

In inviting people to be a part of the parish evangelisation team, you should have had a chance to explain many of the things mentioned above. You may need to run through them again briefly when your team gathers for its first meeting.

In general try to meet in a comfortable environment that is conducive to discussion, reflection and prayer. Provide simple refreshments for everyone: tea, coffee or a soft drink. Be conscious of the fact that if your parish has more than one Mass at the weekend, you are likely to have as many different communities as you have Sunday Masses, and so you will need to provide an opportunity for everyone to introduce themselves to the other members of the team.

Use Chapter One as the basis for reflecting where we as a Church have come from, especially in terms of a growing awareness of the importance of sharing our faith and spreading the Good News.

Read the following passage of scripture, and then as a group discuss its implications for your parish community.

Go, therefore, make disciples of all the nations; baptise them in the name of the Father and of the Son and of the Holy Spirit, and teach them to observe all the commands I gave you. And know that I am with you always; yes, to the end of time. (Matthew 28: 19-20)

Suggested discussion starters:

- What does it mean for us to make disciples of all nations?
- What does it mean for us to know that Jesus is with us always?

Second formation meeting

Use Chapter Two, *Where we are now*, as the basis for this meeting. Look at the following passage, taken from that chapter, and reflect on the implications for your parish.

In the closing homily of the Synod on 28 October 2012, Pope Benedict developed three pastoral themes which he felt came through from the Synod discussions. They can be summarised as follows:

1. *The sacraments of Christian initiation, and the appropriate catechesis for their reception will support people as they encounter the Lord's call to holiness, something which is addressed to all Christians.*
2. *The Church's task is to evangelise, to proclaim the message of salvation to those who do not yet know Jesus Christ. We need to pray for the Holy Spirit to arouse a new missionary dynamism in the Church, involving all members of the Church.*
3. *The baptised who do not live as followers of Christ should be a particular concern, so that they can encounter Jesus Christ anew, rediscover the joy of faith and return to a practice of the faith in the community of the church.*

Suggested discussion starters

- What is the quality of preparation for the sacraments of initiation in our parish? Have those people who are delivering them been prepared for the task and are they well resourced?
- How can we encounter those who do not know Jesus Christ?
- How can we as a parish community help people to rediscover the joy of the Gospel?

Third formation meeting
Use Chapter Three, *Pope Francis*, Evangelii Gaudium and *the parish response* as the basis for discussion.

Fourth formation meeting
Use Chapter Five, *Let's get started*, as a basis for discussion. Use the parish audit contained in that chapter.

Fifth formation meeting
Use Chapter Seven, *Challenges facing every parish* as a basis for this meeting.

The use of material presented in that chapter can help to initiate the discussion on how we proclaim the Gospel message in a world that would appear to be interested more in material things than religious. It can help the team to look at how we respond to the challenge of being a Church filled with a new missionary dynamism.

Suggested discussion starters

- What can we as a parish do to get our message about the joy of the Gospel into our local community?

"What does it mean for us to know that Jesus is with us always?"

- How can we as a parish rediscover and return to the simple, basic announcement of Jesus Christ that is at the heart of our Christian faith?

A prayer for the new evangelisation
The team can adopt or adapt the following as their prayer during its time of formation. This is taken from the end of *Evangelii Gaudium*:

Mary, Virgin and Mother,
you who, moved by the Holy Spirit,
welcomed the word of life
in the depths of your humble faith:
as you gave yourself completely to the Eternal One,
help us to say our own "yes"
to the urgent call, as pressing as ever,
to proclaim the good news of Jesus.

Filled with Christ's presence,
you brought joy to John the Baptist,
making him exult in the womb of his mother.
Brimming over with joy,
you sang of the great things done by God.

Standing at the foot of the cross
with unyielding faith,
you received the joyful comfort of the resurrection,
and joined the disciples in awaiting the Spirit
so that the evangelising Church might be born.

Obtain for us now a new ardour born of the resurrection,
that we may bring to all the Gospel of life
which triumphs over death.
Give us a holy courage to seek new paths,
that the gift of unfading beauty
may reach every man and woman.

Virgin of listening and contemplation,
Mother of love, Bride of the eternal wedding feast,
pray for the Church, whose pure icon you are,
that she may never be closed in on herself
or lose her passion for establishing God's kingdom.

Star of the new evangelisation,
help us to bear radiant witness to communion,
service, ardent and generous faith,
justice and love of the poor,
that the joy of the Gospel
may reach to the ends of the earth,
illuminating even the fringes of our world.

Mother of the living Gospel,
wellspring of happiness for God's little ones,
pray for us.
Amen. Alleluia!

CHAPTER SEVEN

Challenges facing every parish

"The church is the house where the doors are always open not only to welcome everyone in to breathe love and hope, but also so we can take this love and hope outside" (EG, 47)

In a recent YouGov poll for *The Sun* (taken on Easter Saturday, 2012) the National Secular Society questioned 1,742 people regarding their views on Easter worship. The outcome suggested an increasing level of disengagement and ignorance concerning the religious celebration of Easter.

According to this poll, Easter's religious meaning is important to only seventeen percent of Britons, while forty-three percent of people questioned said it was important to spend time with family and friends. Only two percent thought the idea of exchanging Easter eggs was a good one.

The clear majority, seventy-nine percent of those polled, had no plans to go to church over the Easter period; sixteen percent thought they might, with five percent uncertain. On previous form it is highly unlikely, says the report, that the intentions of the sixteen percent would be translated into action.

Weddings and funerals excluded, twelve percent of the respondents claimed to be regular (monthly or more) churchgoers, with twenty percent going very occasionally and sixty-six percent going never or less than once a year.

Among those polled fifty-four percent said they never prayed; nineteen percent claimed that they prayed on a daily or near daily basis; forty-nine percent were adamant that prayer is ineffective; thirty-one percent believed that prayer actually works; twenty-four percent were unsure.

A significant majority – eighty-seven percent – considered Britain to be less religious than fifty years ago.

In another Easter-related poll commissioned, somewhat surprisingly, by Travelodge in March 2013, two thousand families were interviewed about Easter and religious practice. Of those polled, forty percent said they had no interest in the religious side of Easter; twenty-eight percent said they would observe Good Friday as a fast day. A clear majority – eighty-two percent – had no intention of going to church. Among children, fifty-three percent did not know the meaning of Easter, and a quarter thought it was about celebrating the Easter Bunny's birthday.

Clearly, as Christians in this secular world, there is a challenge: should we allow others to hijack the greatest celebration in the Christian calendar and use it to their own ends?

From an evangelising point of view, the answer must be – "Yes!" If we take the view that every opportunity is an opportunity to evangelise – as with St Patrick's Day, for example, when the whole world suddenly re-discovers their Irish roots – then who knows who might come to realise the true meaning of Easter?

Also, if we "allow" non-Christians to celebrate Easter, then this enables us to use the occasion as an opportunity to share the story and memories of Jesus' life with non-believers.

The treasures of inculturation

The central mission of the Church is to spread the Good News of Jesus Christ. As Catholics, this is also our personal mission and responsibility.

In the past this mission was concentrated in far-off lands and focused on indigenous people whose culture was very different to ours. Missionaries, where they were effective, evangelised through a process of inculturation.

The 16th century Italian Jesuit missionary to China, Matteo Ricci, succeeded where others failed. On his arrival

A flicker of faith

Recently a close friend of ours died suddenly. He was a "resting Catholic" and his wife was a practical atheist. We arrived at the hospital just minutes after he passed way: the shock was devastating for us all. After a few moments his wife turned to us and said, "At this moment, I wish I had what you have, faith, but I haven't. You see I believe that he has gone, and that I will never see him again." She paused and then added, "I know that he hadn't been to church in many years but he was brought up a Catholic, so I think for his sake we better have a Catholic funeral, just in case I'm wrong and you lot are right." Is there a flicker of faith there? At the time this friend recognised what a gift faith really is; this gave us an opportunity to reach out to her at a time of loss.

in Macau, he dressed like a Chinese intellectual, learned to read, write and speak Mandarin and spent many years absorbing Chinese culture. His missionary effectiveness arose from his learning to cherish the civilisation into which he became inserted. He could relate with people on their own terms and in accordance with their own traditions and way of life.

Ricci interpreted Jesus and the Gospels into Chinese, not just through translation of texts, but also because he practised what he preached. It is for this reason that, four hundred years after his death, Ricci still sets a prime example of the effectiveness of inculturation.

Inculturation in our parish practice

These days our focus is more localised and we are called to bring the Good News into a more materialistic world whose needs have changed. In this world our lives are driven by a secular need for belonging; every day in our parishes we can meet people who, as mentioned previously, come back to church because, "our parents did it for us" or "it's what we do in our family". They want baptism for their baby because it fulfils an inherent need in them for the ritual as a 'rite of passage', and this can also be said of other sacraments. Finally, many want "the good send-off" of a Catholic funeral.

Inculturation is not necessarily linked to ethnicity or to new arrivals: young people, parents, the elderly and parish groups all have their own culture which needs to be integrated into the uniqueness of the parish. How might we enable this to happen?

Challenges for the Church and the parish

Opportunities for evangelisation emerge from the secular environment of today's world.

Cardinal Donald Wuerl, pictured right, the relator-general of the 2012 Synod on the New Evangelisation, wrote in his report before the discussions:

Entire generations have become disassociated from the support systems that facilitated the transmission of faith. It is as if a tsunami of secular influence has swept across the cultural landscape, taking with it such social markers as marriage, family, the concept of the common good and objective right and wrong…

The missionaries in the first Evangelisation covered immense geographic distances to spread the Good News. We, the missionaries of the New Evangelisation, must surmount ideological distances just as immense, often times before we ever journey beyond our own neighbourhood or family…

In November 2012, Cardinal Donald Wuerl spoke at a meeting at the Catholic Evangelisation Centre in Washington DC. The Catholic News Agency reported him saying:

The New Evangelisation is the Church's response to the secularism, materialism and individualism that have swept across Western culture… and washed away the things that had been part of the fabric of society, such as the moral order and common good…

> *"Without Christ, the Christian mandate to share the message of salvation in Jesus is an impossible mission."*

The Church is called to return to the simple, basic announcement of Jesus Christ that is at the heart of the Christian faith. This task of passing on the Good News of Christ involves all Catholics and must begin with family, and begins with Baptism.

Our parishes have the central role in evangelising because it is there that we encounter the results of our secular society. This meeting might be through a couple requesting baptism for their child, a family wanting a Catholic funeral for a lapsed relative, a couple wanting to marry but finding themselves in a difficult situation, or a homeless young person looking for help. Each situation presents us with the opportunity to bring the Good News of Christ to them and to let them know and feel the loving support that comes only with knowing the Lord. Even if we cannot give each individual the answer they want, we must ask ourselves: "Can we offer them what Jesus would have offered them?"

Cardinal Wuerl, in his Washington comments on the 2012 Synod, said:

The message begins with the Gospel story about the Samaritan woman who meets Jesus at the well and is instantly transformed… The sinner who was converted becomes a messenger of salvation and leads the whole city to Jesus… Without Christ, the Christian mandate to share the message of salvation in Jesus is an impossible mission.

Crossing the Threshold

Between 2011-2013, the Home Mission desk of the Bishops' Conference of England and Wales, initiated a nationwide programme entitled *Crossing the Threshold*. This highlighted the fact that we have to cross the threshold in order to reach out to others. For their part, others must be invited to cross the threshold if they are to experience the life of the Church and how we worship together.

At the launch conference, Archbishop Bernard Longley of Birmingham, speaking about the opportunity the Year of Faith presented, commented:

The Year of Faith will help us to recapture something of the richness of our faith as it is expressed in the Catechism of the Catholic Church. It should encourage us to re-equip ourselves to take the message and the example of faith to those whose faith has grown weaker or who have drifted away from the Church for whatever reason…

The New Evangelisation is not only for Europe but is especially for places where secularisation has changed people's experience and practice of faith.

We should be cautious not to adopt a wholly negative attitude towards secularism and we should distinguish it from secularisation. Secularism can certainly have some negative impacts but the phenomenon can also offer a new freedom for the Gospel to be proclaimed.

Bishop Edwin Regan of Wrexham remarked:

Only God can call people back to the practice of their faith, from whatever was dead in their past lives. Only God can forgive sins – but we can play our part, and be part of the invitation to cross the threshold, to unbind them and set them free.

Pope Francis used the guidance of Matthew, Mark, Luke and John to write his Apostolic Exhortation, *Evangelii Gaudium*. Throughout this book, our focus has also been to use the word of God as our manual to help you and your fellow parishioners to become an evangelising parish.

The parish as a centre for evangelisation

Writing about the importance of the parish, Pope Francis states:

The parish is not an outdated institution… it continues to be "the Church living in the midst of the homes of her sons and daughters"… In all its activities the parish encourages and trains its members to be evangelisers. It is a community of communities, a sanctuary where the thirsty come to drink in the midst of their journey and a centre of constant missionary outreach…

The parish is the presence of the Church in a given territory, an environment for hearing God's word, for growth in the Christian life, for dialogue, proclamation, charitable outreach, worship and celebration. In all its activities the parish encourages and trains its members to be evangelisers. It is a community of communities, a sanctuary where the thirsty come to drink in the midst of their journey, and a centre of constant missionary outreach. We must admit, though, that the call to review and renew our parishes has not yet sufficed to bring them nearer to people, to make them environments of living communion and participation, and to make them completely mission-oriented. (EG, 28)

And on secularisation Pope Francis writes:

The process of secularisation tends to reduce the faith and the Church to the sphere of the private and personal. Furthermore, by completely rejecting the transcendent, it has produced a growing deterioration of ethics, a weakening of the sense of personal and collective sin, and a steady increase in relativism. These have led to a general sense of disorientation, especially in the periods of adolescence and young adulthood which are so vulnerable to change... We are living in an information-driven society which bombards us indiscriminately with data – all treated as being of equal importance – and which leads to remarkable superficiality in the area of moral discernment. In response, we need to provide an education which teaches critical thinking and encourages the development of mature moral values. (EG, 64)

"In all its activities the parish encourages and trains its members to be evangelisers."

In the modern world secularisation is seen as being non-religious and inculturation as being at one with our cultural surroundings. If we embrace these ideals then non-believers would take the view that this equates to freedom. However, there is an argument that this is only a short journey to totalitarianism, a phenomenon that is enforced not always through the workings of a revolutionary state, but through a modern cultural need to make our own choices, between religion and secularism.

Secularist would argue that religion enforces its own belief system on a person and consequently our freedom is diminished. However, as society becomes increasingly more complex, and populations prosper, so does our freedom to make choices. More and more, our choices become materialistic and we drift into a situation where secular culture dominates our choices and the decisions that govern our lives.

Dr Jeff Mirus, the founder of CatholicCulture.org writes:

Secularism! While the totalitarian impulse can be found in some religions, it is generally held strongly in check by Christianity. This is because Christianity holds that every human person is made in the image and likeness of God, which means a reasonable degree of self-determination is part of his dignity; and also because Christianity holds that a perfect world is not possible here on earth. Rather, we are to live now according to the law of love so as to be worthy of perfection in the next life. Secularism has neither restraint. It lacks a coherent understanding of human dignity, and it is intrinsically (and often desperately) ordered toward utopianism. The secularist has but one shot at the world he wants. Hence secularism, which begins in proclaiming freedom from God, always ends by enslaving the mass of men under the program of its visionaries.
(Secularism, Acculturation and Creeping Totalitarianism, CatholicCulture.org 5 May 2008)

Having attended several humanist funerals, the words of Dr Mirus resonate for both of us: "The secularist has but one shot at the world he wants." We all know someone who does not believe in life after death. Our faith and the Gospel message are the only tools we have to help non-believers understand that Jesus Christ died and rose again, so that we might have life and live it to the full. To do this we need to embrace secular culture and use it as a tool to bring the love of God to those who do not yet believe, bringing them the hope of eternal life.

Move a little closer

One night in Advent, during one of the sessions we were leading in a local prison, we noticed that the prison officer sat quite a distance away from the group of prisoners. As the session progressed, watching a section of a film and then discussing it, the officer actually moved his chair closer to the group and began to listen into the discussion. In a world where many people would say that there is no interest in God and religion, that experience made us reflect on the fact that it's about what we offer and how we present it that can lead to drawing people into a discussion.

CHAPTER EIGHT

How to use the new social media for evangelisation

Good communication helps us to grow closer, to know one another better and, ultimately, to grow in unity

(Pope Francis, Message for the 48th World Communications Day, 1 June 2014)

As it was

Strange as it might seem, in past centuries ships made use of a "letter box" as they travelled around the Cape of Good Hope at the southern tip of what is today South Africa. The "letter box" was marked by a large stone which the crew of any passing ship checked. An international unwritten agreement meant that letters could be left and collected for delivery to the nearest port to their intended destination. The average time between posting and delivery was between three and six years. Writing by "return of post" meant something completely different to the system which we take for granted in today's world.

As it is

The Good News does not change. The new evangelisation is not about a new message. The call to new evangelisation is about the challenge to find new methods of transmitting the Good News in our current culture and society.

If we do not make use of the incredible recent advances in communications in our service of the Gospel, then we limit our outreach and effectiveness.

In his message for World Communications Day 2014, Pope Francis commended the widespread availability of Internet access. Describing it as offering "immense possibilities for encounter and solidarity", he added that it is "something truly good, a gift from God".

The ability to communicate through technology is a vast human achievement, its rapid growth challenging the Church to adopt the best in its service of transmitting our faith in the Gospel message.

Let us look at some of the new technologies that we could harness in the service of the Gospel and the new evangelisation.

Twitter

In our own parish, we are most definitely converts to the world of Twitter and are filled with enthusiasm for its newly-discovered opportunities.

One of our parishioners recently promised to "set it all up" and to teach us how to use it. We entered, somewhat nervously, into this new world of Twitter.

We encouraged members of the parish to follow us on Twitter, and we began tweeting. At first only twenty or so people followed us, but then the numbers gradually increased. Today, more than a hundred people follow the parish Twitter account (which, for a parish, we feel is a good number).

What do we use it for? Firstly, from the very outset, it was not the parish priest's personal Twitter account but the parish's. This means that it refers to parish events and parish outreach, rather than what the parish priest had for lunch! When illness suddenly prevented us from leading a "Seeking Christ" group meeting, we were able to tweet that the meeting was cancelled and the message prevented group members from making an unnecessary journey and the meeting was re-scheduled.

Below are a few of the ways in which we use it.

• **Baptisms**
Each week when we celebrate the sacrament of baptism, we tweet a message after the ceremony, asking people to pray for the newly baptised. We also welcome them as new members of the Church and of our parish. These messages are usually re-tweeted by the families of the person baptised.

• **Weddings**
The day before a wedding we tweet asking people to keep the couple in their prayers on their wedding day. As soon as the wedding service is completed, we take a photograph of the couple. Before they reach the venue for their reception, we have already tweeted the photograph and a message of congratulations. The couple's family and friends rapidly re-tweet the text and the picture.

"Some parishioners have suggested that the homily at Sunday Mass should be the size of a tweet – 140 characters maximum!"

• **Funerals**
The day before a funeral and again on the day of a parish funeral, we tweet, asking people to remember the deceased in their prayers. Many people, including the bereaved family receive and re-tweet these prayer requests and so the circle of prayer extends.

• **Sacramental landmarks**
Throughout the year, we celebrate sacramental milestones in the life of our younger parishioners, such as their presentation for the sacraments of confirmation and first communion. These are important moments when we ask people to pray for the children.

• **Parish pilgrimages**
Twitter keeps the parish in touch during any parish or diocesan pilgrimage. We post photographs and news updates. Many of our followers reply to us during the pilgrimages and re-tweet our communications.

• **Social events**
We also tweet about the social occasions when we come together as a parish, purely to enjoy each other's company: Burns' Night, St Patrick's Night, St George's Night, our annual parish fun sports day and our breakfast on "Welcome Sunday" on the First Sunday of Advent – all these generate their own tweets.

These short messages (some parishioners have suggested that the homily at Sunday Mass should be the size of a tweet – one hundred and forty characters maximum!) send out a message of a community that celebrates welcoming new members, rejoices with others on the occasion of life-changing events, and also encourages prayers for parishioners and world events.

Each of our followers has his or her own followers, so that, when a tweet is re-tweeted the message reaches even more people.

But it is not only about what we tweet. We also follow what others tweet. It is a perfect tool for a speedy check on world events and especially helpful in supplying a short inspirational thought for the daily homily. Most of Pope Francis' morning homilies in the Vatican are tweeted by the time we have our daily Mass!

Despite our initial reluctance to use Twitter, we now see it as a tool for the new evangelisation which also includes the younger generation in its outreach.

As well as working in the parish, we also run the Department for Evangelisation in our diocese; we are now gradually building on our parish experience of Twitter. A tweet has a faster and wider outreach than a leaflet or newsletter advertising forthcoming events or resources.

Facebook

A Facebook page is another tool in the work of the new evangelisation. Again there will be several questions that you need to ask, such as: why create a Facebook page? How do you do it? Who will maintain it? What do you post to it? It is important to seek advice from those who understand these things (usually the younger members of our communities), and then enlist their help in setting up and maintaining the page.

A Facebook page provides a parish with several benefits. Firstly, it is an additional avenue to communicate with your parish and beyond. With more than five hundred million users worldwide – many in your parish

community already have their own Facebook account – Facebook users are typically loyal, checking and updating their page daily.

You will need to decide who will create the page initially and who will be the administrator. It is useful to have a couple of people as administrators in order to monitor and keep posts and interactions lively. So what do you post on your page? It can be used for a variety of purposes and here are some ideas:

- photographs of events
- announcements of events and links to more information

- link to a blog post from your clergy to ask a question or initiate a thought – a great way to start a conversation
- videos or articles you find relating to the faith
- daily readings and reflections

The Internet and parish websites

Most important: The website needs to be maintained, kept up-to-date and relevant. The latest parish newsletter should be the one people can download on a particular Sunday, not one from three months or three years previously!

Something to share: Others outside your own local community can see that you have something to share.

Once again it has to be said that a parish website is just that: the parish's website and not the parish priest's website!

Involving young people: A parish website can be a great way of involving younger parishioners in its building and maintenance.

Information at a touch: The daily Mass schedule for the current week needs to be accessible. Contact information, ministries and groups must be correct and up-to-date.

Vibrancy and outreach: The parish website is a great tool for indicating the vibrancy of a parish community.

People other than your own parishioners will discover your website, in a sense, by accident. Several years ago, someone in Florida, who had emigrated to the States many years ago, contacted us through our parish website, curious to know about our local grammar school she had attended. We were able to update her and also to arrange for her to visit the parish and her former school on her next visit to the UK. We all forged new and lasting relationships.

Welcoming and inviting: Encourage people to visit the parish if they are in the vicinity. Tell them how to find the church (especially important if you are not on a main road, but in the middle of a housing estate or heavily built-up area). Give a contact name and the all-important telephone number.

Content guidelines: Follow your diocesan safeguarding guidelines, especially in relation to personal telephone numbers and photographs. We never publish photographs that identify any specific person, unless they are a member of staff in the parish. All invitations to contact a particular group or ministry are always directed through the parish office.
In short, keep your parish website current, informative, attractive, and easy to navigate.

> *"A parish website can be a great way of involving younger parishioners in its building and maintenance."*

A good general rule is that you should need no more than three clicks of the computer mouse to be in the place you want to be on any website. Any more than three and people lose interest. You could lose a valuable opportunity to reach out to someone through your website.

Pope Francis, in his 2014 Message for World Communication Sunday, comments that:

By means of the Internet, the Christian message can reach 'to the ends of the earth' (Acts 1:8). Keeping the doors of our churches open also means keeping them open in the digital environment so that people, whatever their situation in life, can enter, and so that the Gospel can go out to reach everyone.

E-mails

Messages: Many people now use e-mails as their main method of communication, often accessing their e-mails wherever they are. If you have a parish e-mail address, is the inbox regularly checked? If not, it is as useful as an out-of-date website – of no use!

Weekly e-newsletter: It is such a simple thing, but it keeps people in touch with the parish community and the latest news. We have found that former parishioners who have moved away from the area are keen to keep up with what is happening in the parish. We find that, as some of our parishioners find it more difficult to get out each week to Mass, especially during a harsh winter, they like to receive the newsletter by e-mail. Students who have gone to university keep in touch with us through receiving the newsletter each week by e-mail, and on many occasions, family members of our parishioners, who live away from our area, also receive it.

To set this up was incredibly simple. We created a distribution group in our e-mail address book, adding the addresses of parishioners who wanted to receive the weekly e-newsletter. As soon as the newsletter is completed each week, we create a pdf document, attach it to the distribution group of e-mail addresses, and send it out with one click of a mouse. It is all done in about the same amount of time it takes to print the first five copies.

The parish newsletter

In many ways what we have encouraged about the parish website can be said for the weekly newsletter – make it current, informative, attractive, and easy to navigate. Re-create its design at least once a year; move and change items every few weeks; plan content; ensure that there is always something that is going to enrich the reader's faith; help them to reflect on the Sunday scripture readings. They may not remember the powerful homily delivered at Mass, but most people will take the newsletter home with them, and read it that day or during the week – unless of course they have read it during the wonderfully powerful homily itself!

"Why not ask someone in the parish to be the parish information officer?"

Of course, the extraordinary ministers of the Eucharist who take communion to the sick and house-bound are a very real link with the parish. They should take a newsletter to give to those whom they visit. We also print a good number of large print newsletters for the visually impaired in our community.

The local newspaper and local radio

Are you ever frustrated when it seems that almost everything that happened at St Swithin's church makes it into the local newspaper and radio, but nothing that

your parish organises or does ever appears in this media? Why? Ask yourself the question: Do you tell them?

Local newspapers and local radio stations are crying out for local news. This is what sells the papers and maintains audience ratings. Why not ask someone in the parish to be the parish information officer? Their role would be to e-mail or post the weekly newsletter to the local press and radio station. Follow them on Twitter or Facebook and re-tweet a good tweet. This draws their attention to the fact that you are a follower. They might then begin to start following you in the hope of good nuggets of information or a story. Identify someone in your parish, who is able to talk to them. Do not be afraid of the media. They can help to share the good news of what we, a welcoming and inviting Christian community, are doing in our neighbourhood. The local media needs our "good news stories".

Your local newspaper and radio station can be a great way of spreading the Good News in this time of the new evangelisation. Many local radio stations have a dedicated faith programme, often on Sunday mornings. Our own local radio station has around forty thousand people listening to the Sunday morning faith programme. If you have the chance to get on there, grab it!

There are more opportunities than ever before for the Church to share the Good News. Are we, as parish communities, making the most of them, even imitating in our own small way the Vatican's own use of the new social media?

As Pope Francis said:

The Church needs to be concerned for, and present in, the world of communication, in order to dialogue with people today and to help them encounter Christ. She needs to be a Church at the side of others, capable of accompanying everyone along the way. The revolution taking place in communications media and in information technologies represents a great and thrilling challenge; may we respond to that challenge with fresh energy and imagination as we seek to share with others the beauty of God. (Message for the 48th World Communications Day 2014)

"Our own local radio station has around forty thousand people listening to the Sunday morning faith programme. If you have the chance to get on there, grab it!"

CHAPTER NINE

Looking around at other faiths

Towards today

In May 2014 Pope Francis stood at the Western Wall in the heart of Jerusalem and prayed for peace and reconciliation in the world. His companions at the Wall were his old friends Rabbi Abraham Skorka and Muslim leader Omar Abboud. After praying the Our Father he observed the Jewish tradition of placing a written prayer in a niche in the wall. Never before has it been possible for these three leaders to talk so openly and frankly. This could not have been brought about without the mutual respect that these three faith leaders have for each other and their ultimate desire for peace in the world.

Evangelisation and witness

The aims of evangelisation and its relationship with and to other faiths are:

- To work for understanding between people of faith
- To learn about the beliefs and practices of different religions
- To be equipped to talk about our own faith

Increasingly, we live in a society where our neighbours may not worship the same way as we do, or on the same day. They might not even recognise the same Supreme Being. These days our neighbours may well go to the mosque or temple on Friday or to the synagogue on Saturday: this is what we have come to expect in our multicultural and multi-religious society. This mix of ethnicity has enriched our culture and given us a greater understanding of our

mission to bring the Good News to the people around us. Gone are the days when Jesuit theologian Karl Rahner (1904-1984) spent time and energy arguing about his controversial notion of "the anonymous Christian". Stephen Clinton, in his book *Peter, Paul, and the Anonymous Christian: A Response to the Mission Theology of Rahner and Vatican ll,* quotes Rahner as declaring that "people who have never heard the Christian Gospel might be saved through Christ…non-Christians have, in their basic orientation, a fundamental decision to accept the salvific grace of God, through Christ, although they may never have heard of the Christian revelation."

At the time this was felt to be too radical and Rahner was reprimanded for his hypothesis by the Catholic Church. If Rahner were alive today, would he be the one at the forefront of interreligious dialogue?

When we witness to our faith, we do so in many different ways. Our prayer and liturgy help us to celebrate who we are and what we believe. They help to define us as Catholics. They are not meant to be tools for drawing people into the faith.

In his message marking the fiftieth anniversary of the Pontifical Council for Interreligious Dialogue, Pope Francis compared the Church's willingness to engage with people of other religions to Christ's journey on the road to Emmaus. "Such a willingness to walk together is all the more necessary in our time."

Evangelisation and dialogue

Successful dialogue only happens in openness and willingness to listen to someone else's point of view. Dialogue demands and builds trust, even when its participants eventually "agree to differ".

In his Encyclical *Redemptoris Missio,* St John Paul II wrote:

In the light of the economy of salvation, the Church sees no conflict between proclaiming Christ and engaging in interreligious dialogue. Instead, she feels the need to link the two in the context of her mission ad gentes. (RM, 55)

When Jesus said: "I am the way, the truth and the life", he did not specify a particular group of recipients. He did not stipulate that he is "the way, the truth and the life for Christians, Muslims, Hindus or Jews".

Interreligious dialogue and the parish

Every parish needs the richness that interreligious dialogue brings to our Christian and, more importantly, Catholic community.

"When I go out to the villages to say Mass, I have often had Hindus and Muslims coming to complain that I had spoken to the Catholics and not to them. 'You are speaking of values', they said, 'and they are values that we share. When you come here, we want you to speak of those values to all of us and not just to the Catholics.'"

The Indian Jesuit who spoke these words was describing his situation in India. Yet his words are equally applicable across the world. People of all religions and none share certain values. Today's world is often torn by misunderstanding and division. People of faith need to draw closer in supportive understanding if there is to be hope for humanity.

Meeting God in Friend and Stranger

In England and Wales, a defining moment in the

history of inter-faith dialogue happened in 2010 with the publication of *Meeting God in Friend and Stranger*. This was a teaching document from the Catholic Bishops' Conference of England and Wales on relations between the Catholic Church and other religions.

But even earlier, on 28 October 1965, Pope Paul VI promulgated the *Declaration on the Relations of the Church to other non-Christian Religions*. This document, called *Nostra Aetate*, was a Vatican Council document; it opened:

In our time, when day by day mankind is being drawn closer together, and the ties between different people are becoming stronger, the Church examines more closely her relationship with other non-Christian religions. In her task of promoting love and unity among men, indeed, nations, she considers above all in this declaration what men have in common and what draws them to fellowship.

This decree was to turn the tide of inter-faith relations, especially between the Jewish and Catholic traditions, bringing with it a new, fresh understanding of each other and an openness to dialogue. This was followed on the ninth anniversary of the promulgation of *Nostra Aetate* by guidelines and suggestions for implementing this conciliar declaration.

The Jewish response to this document was published some thirty-five years later in September 2000, entitled *Dabru Emet: a Jewish statement on Christians and Christianity*. It observed:

Jews and Christians worship the same God. Before the rise of Christianity, Jews were the only worshippers of the God of Israel. But Christians also worship the God of Abraham, Isaac, and Jacob; creator of heaven and earth. While Christian worship is not a viable religious choice for Jews,

"Successful dialogue only happens in openness and willingness to listen to someone else's point of view."

as Jewish theologians we rejoice that, through Christianity, hundreds of millions of people have entered into relationship with the God of Israel. (DE, 1)

In *Evangelii Gaudium* Pope Francis wrote: "I invite everyone to be bold and creative in this task of rethinking the goals, structures, styles and methods of evangelisation in their respective communities." (*EG*, 33)

Interfaith dialogue and our parish

Many of the people around us belong to what are called the Abrahamic Faiths: Judaism, Christianity and Islam. In other words, they look back in time to Abraham as their "father in faith". In focusing on inter-faith dialogue in relation to larger ethnic group within our areas, we can suggest a programme that is a guide for future initiatives with peoples of all groups and faiths.

(To assist you with these issues we suggest spending one evening over coffee and refreshments just examining your parish area and highlighting which groups are more prominent within the parish boundaries.)

INTERRELIGIOUS DIALOGUE AND OUR PARISH

Looking around at other faiths
Welcome to these discussions.
The aims are simple, so that the people of our parish will be able to:

- recognise the common origins of the faiths surrounding our parish

- celebrate the shared values and the differences
- compare and contrast Judaism, Christianity and Islam
- evaluate the current relations between Jews, Christians and Muslims
- reflect upon the contents of these sessions and communicate with others

Which religions describe themselves as "Abrahamic"?
Why do they give themselves this name?
Why do Jews not have meat and milk at the same time?
What is the name of the Muslim call to prayer?
Why do Sikh men wear turbans?
Which religions do not allow their followers to eat pork?
What animal is sacred to a Hindu?

Which is the most commonly practiced religion in this area?
What is the difference between a religion and a denomination?
Do our parishioners meet people of other religions?
Could our parish organise an event with a group from one or more other religions?
What could we do?

Can you identify the religion and its symbol?
What is the meaning of the symbol?
What do these religions call their Holy Book?

Let's take a closer look at the Abrahamic faiths

To be able to dialogue with other faiths we need to understand more about them. To assist our parish to a greater understanding of the foundations of Islam and Judaism here is a useful *Question and Answer* session. It will give some insight into the differences and similarities between the three Abrahamic faiths and bring a greater understanding of the three faiths to parishioners wishing to pursue the work of evangelisation in an inter-faith context.

The following is a suggested structure:

By looking at the Abrahamic faiths and the significance of Abraham in each, we can recognise the possibilities of Abraham as a unifying factor for the three faiths.

THE ABRAHAMIC FAITHS

JUDAISM CHRISTIANITY ISLAM

What day of the week is holy?

What is the place of worship called?

Name at least one feast.

What is the Holy Book called?

Why are all three religions sometimes called "the people of the Book"?

Why is Abraham important?

How do Judaism and Islam differ in their relationship to Abraham?

What is the name of their religious law?

Name at least one place which is holy to each religion.

DISCUSSION QUESTIONS

- How does each faith understand God?
- What is important about the Jewish, Christian and Muslim understanding of Abraham?
- Can the figure of Abraham unite the three religions? How?
- Why is Jerusalem special to each religion?

In a guest lecture for the Salford Department of Evangelisation, Dr Kessler of the Woolf Institute for Abrahamic Faiths, Cambridge, said: "Visiting each other's sacred space could be regarded as a triumph for interfaith dialogue." Could you arrange a parish visit to a local mosque and synagogue?

Contemporary encounter and the challenge for the future:

- How do we engender more trust among the three faiths? Particularly how do we promote intra-community awareness of the suffering of the other?
- Try to develop programmes for interfaith reading of sacred texts to educate, inform and deepen our understanding of one another.
- The three faiths need to share with each other their understandings of peace and spirituality.
- Through dialogue each community can articulate what it needs from the other two communities.
- Try to arrange visits to each other's place of worship.

(Information to assist with these sessions can be obtained in the resource section at the end of the book.)

As we saw earlier, the work of evangelisation in an inter-faith context does not take on a proselytising character but one of dialogue, aimed at leading us to a greater understanding of each other. Through this we, as Catholics, can gain a greater understanding of ourselves.

Being invited into the "sacred space" of others

The work of evangelisation is very varied and one of the aspects of this work is the dialogue we have with those of other faiths. Over the years we have developed links with many people who work within these communities and who are involved in forging links between various communities and promoting understanding with all cultures. We have arranged courses and talks throughout the diocese and we have gained much from the many friendships we have formed. A couple of years ago we were blessed with an invitation to the bat-mitzvah of Ellie, the youngest child of Ed and Trish Kessler. This was a marvellous day and we were honoured to be included in this special occasion and to be welcomed warmly into the sacredness of this day. This is what inter faith dialogue is about, being welcomed into the sacred space of another and being able to experience what brings us all together.

Pope Francis puts this into context in *Evangelii Gaudium* when he says:

God continues to work among the people of the Old Covenant and to bring forth treasures of wisdom which flow from their encounter with his word. For this reason, the Church also is enriched when she receives the values of Judaism. (EG, 249)

ChameleonsEye / Shutterstock.com

CONCLUSION

Drawing it all together

I have come so that they may have life and have it to the full

(John 10:10)

In this book, we have tried to illustrate the development of the Church's own understanding of the nature of evangelisation in today's world. We are entering a new era in the life of the church with a growing awareness that there is now a new urgency about the necessity to evangelise.

We have tried to look at evangelisation from different aspects of the life of the Church. We have focussed on the parish community and the lives of the individuals who make up the Church. We hope that the ideas and materials that we have shared with you will be of use in moving forward from being a welcoming parish to a witnessing and inviting parish.

Jesus came so that all people might have life and have it to the full. As Christians we believe that we have that life. We must therefore imitate Jesus in wanting to share that abundance with everyone we encounter.

In the course of our work we meet many people in parishes who worry about the lack of young people in our churches and ask what we can do about it. It is interesting that people very rarely comment on the lack of older people or middle-aged people who are just as obvious by their absence! We have to reach out to all age-groups and invite them to come and see what we have discovered as the expression of the fullness of life in Jesus Christ.

We must also be realistic. Some of the factors that are leading people away from the Church are beyond our control. Take young people, for example: many of them distrust all institutions and not just religious ones! Yet, at the same time, there are places and churches where an increased number of young people attend and play an active part.

But not all factors are beyond our control. That is why we must examine them and then work on those we can change.

For example, people like "local" in their search for food, shops, schools, doctor and entertainment. We all like to make friends in the community in which we live. So the Church and our parish must be a vibrant and inviting "meeting place" in the locality, for local people.

Once people have experienced an invitation and a welcome, the experience of community will keep them coming back, hopefully, week after week. People will generally take on responsibility in their parish community when they realise that they are needed. In discovering that their local Church community appreciates their gifts and talents, they have something to offer and use for the good of others.

We will never be done with the work of evangelisation. There will always be people who need our outreach, people with whom we can share the Good News and people who want to experience the fullness of life offered by Jesus Christ. As Christians we live in the world. We must be in dialogue with the world that God loves.

Pope Francis, during his homily at Mass on 15 May 2014, observed that the Church is "a people walking toward fullness; a chosen people which has a promise for the future and walks toward this promise, toward the fulfilment of this promise."

Are we a people walking towards fullness? Are we people filled with hope? Are we willing to walk with people on their journey? That is what evangelisers do as they share the Gospel; this is the kind of people we can all be in our parishes.

Let us be people of hope.

RESOURCES

Resources available through Redemptorist Publications

DVD

New Evangelisation
Archbishop Bernard Longley

BOOKS

**New Evangelisation: What it is &
How to do it**
Fr Stephen Wang
Catholic Truth Society
(2013)

**Catholic Update Guide to the New
Evangelisation**
Mary Carol Kendzia
St Anthony Messenger Press
(2013)

Jesus the Evangelist
Allan F Wright
St Anthony Messenger Press
(2013)

**The Urgency of the New
Evangelisation: Answering the Call**
Ralph Martin
Our Sunday Visitor (2013)

**Parish Guide to the New
Evangelisation: An Action Plan for
Sharing the Faith**
Fr Robert J Hater
Our Sunday Visitor (2013)

**New Evangelisation: Passing on the
Catholic faith today**
Cardinal Donald Wuerl
Our Sunday Visitor (1 Jan 2013)

***Evangelii Gaudium:* a group
reading guide**
Twenty-Third Publications (2014)

Disciples of All Nations
Dr Josephine Lombardi
Twenty-Third Publications
(2014)

Parish Guide to Social Media
Clarissa Valbuena Aljentera
Twenty-Third Publications
(2013)

I Believe: The Creed and you
James Forsyth
Editions Novalis (2012)

25 Questions about....
(series on various topics)
Les Miller Editions Novalis

**Sharing the Faith that You
Love**
John & Therese Boucher
Word Among Us Press (2014)

CHURCH DOCUMENTS

Evangelii Nuntiandi
Pope Paul VI
8 Dec 1975

Redemptoris Missio
St John Paul II
7 Dec 1990

Evangelii Gaudium
Pope Francis
24 Nov 2013

Nostra Aetate
(Declaration on the Relation of
the Church with Non-Christian
Religions of the Second Vatican
Council)
28 October 1965
Vatican II and post-Vatican II
documents

Meeting God in Friend and Stranger
The Catholic Bishops' Conference of England and Wales
ISBN 978 1 86082 663 4 (2010)
Freely available as a pdf from www.catholic-ew.org.uk and other Catholic Internet resources.
Also available from The Catholic Truth Society (2010)

Evangelisation in England & Wales: a report to the Catholic bishops
Philip Knights & Andrea Murray, Catholic Communications Service (2002)
ISBN 090524124X, 9780905241241
Freely available as a pdf from www.catholic-ew.org.uk and other Catholic Internet resources.

RESOURCES AVAILABLE THROUGH THE PAULIST EVANGELIZATION MINISTRIES AND PAULIST PRESS
The Paulist Evangelization Ministries (Washington DC) produce a wide range of excellent evangelisation resources. Full details can be found on their website: http://www.pemdc.org/. They are written primarily for an American readership and may need adaptation for a UK parish. Both programmes need to be ordered through the website as they are not readily available in the UK.

Two programmes from the Paulist Evangelization Ministries (Washington DC):

Seeking Christ
This is an eight-session programme, aimed at providing a resource for parishes, to welcome and engage people who come enquiring about the Catholic faith. Each session involves a short DVD reflection, scripture passage and take-home sheet. This programme can form the enquiry part of RCIA.

Awakening Faith - Reconnecting with Your Catholic Faith
This is a six-session programme that helps inactive Catholics return to the Church. A parish can offer *Awakening Faith* any time of the year and repeat it time and again.

Creating the Evangelising Parish
Frank DeSiano CSP & Kenneth Boyack CSP
Paulist Press (1993)

From Maintenance to Mission
Robert S Rivers CSP
Paulist Press (2005)

The New Catholic Evangelisation
Kenneth Boyack CSP (ed)
Paulist Press (1992)

The New Evangelisation
Steven Boguslawski OP and Ralph Martin (ed)
Paulist Press (2008)

BOOKS FROM AVE MARIA PRESS
Rebuilt – The Story of a Catholic Parish
Michael White and Tom Corcoran
Ave Maria Press, Notre Dame, Indiana (2013)

Tools for Rebuilding – 75 really, really practical ways to make your parish better
Michael White and Tom Corcoran
Ave Maria Press, Notre Dame, Indiana (2013)

SUGGESTED FURTHER READING
Basic Evangelisation
Pat Collins CM
Columba Press (2010)

The Church of Mercy
Pope Francis
Darton, Longman and Todd (2014)

John Paul II and the New Evangelisation
Ralph Martin & Peter Williamson
Servant Books (2006)

The New Evangelisation and You
Greg Willits
Servant Books (2013)

The Urgency of the New Evangelisation: answering the call
Ralph Martin
Our Sunday Visitor (2013)

INTER-FAITH BOOKS
What do Jews Believe?
Dr Edward Kessler
Granta Books (2006)

An Introduction to Jewish, Christian, Muslim Relations
Dr Edward Kessler
Cambridge University Press (2010)

A Very Short Introduction to Judaism
Norman Soloman
OUP Oxford (2000)

A Very Short Introduction to Christianity
Linda Woodhead
OUP Oxford (2004)

A Very Short Introduction to Islam
Malise Ruthven
OUP Oxford (2012)

Buddhism: A Very Short Introduction
Damien Keown
OUP Oxford; second edition (2013)

Sikhism: A Very Short Introduction
Eleanor Nesbitt
OUP Oxford (2005)

Hinduism: A Very Short Introduction
Kim Knott
Oxford Paperbacks; new edition (2000)